WEST
POINT
IN THE MAKING *of*
AMERICA

★ ★ ★ ★ ★

WEST POINT

IN THE MAKING *of*

AMERICA

★ ★ ★ ★ ★

SMITHSONIAN NATIONAL MUSEUM
OF AMERICAN HISTORY

BEHRING CENTER

Foreword by Senator Jack Reed

HYDRA PUBLISHING

HYDRA PUBLISHING
IRVINGTON, NEW YORK

Text: Barton C. Hacker and Margaret Vining, Smithsonian
Institution
Editors: George Ochoa and Melinda Corey
Designer: Claire Legemah
Smithsonian Project Coordinator: Ellen Nanney
Publisher: Sean Moore

First Edition, 2002
2 4 6 8 10 9 7 5 3 1
Published in the United States by
Hydra Publishing
50 Mallard Rise
Irvington, New York 10533

A catalog record for this book is available from the Library of Congress.

ISBN 1-59258-025-4

Printed in China by DNP

Cover: The twentieth panel in the Travis Panorama, painted by William De Laney
Trimble Travis shortly after the Civil War. To get into position to strike at
Confederate general Braxton Bragg, Union general William Starke Rosecrans sends
some of his troops and wagon trains through the widely separated passes of
Lookout Mountain.

Title page: The 4th U.S. Infantry at the Battle of El Molino Del Rey, Mexico,
8 September 1847, as depicted by James Walker in one of his series of Mexican
War paintings

Contents page: West Point from Garrison, New York, c.1920, as painted by
Gifford Beal

CONTENTS

ACKNOWLEDGMENTS

★ This book is a companion to the exhibition *West Point in the Making of America, 1802–1918*, a collective effort of the staff of the Smithsonian Institution's National Museum of American History. Exhibitions are complex undertakings, and the history represented here is an interpretation of historical evidence informed by knowledge and experience.

Curators: Barton Hacker, Margaret Vining
Curatorial Support: Ann Burrola, Kathy Golden, Patricia Jernigan, Mary Mack, David Miller
Editor: Nancy Growald Brooks
Project Manager: Andrew Heymann
Education Advisors: Julia Forbes, Heather Paisley-Jones, Matthew White
Design: PRD Group Ltd.
A/V Production: Pyramid Studios
Web Design & Support: Hello Design; Judith Gradwohl
Fabrication: Explus Incorporated; Valley Craftsmen
Design & Fabrication Support: Peter Albritton, Robbie Barrett, Lou Covey, Joseph Criste, Stevan Fisher, Don Hurlbert, Brian Jensen, Larry Jones, Juan Smith, Richard Strauss, Tom Tearman, Lisa-Renee Thompson, Roger Wright, Omar Wynn
Preservation Support: Sunae Park Evans, Gaby Kienitz, Beth Richwine, Jia-sun Tsang, Catherine Williams, Helen Young
Funds Management & Support: Laura McClure, Zugeily Junier
Registration Services: Tom Bower
Public Affairs: Adrienne Durand
National Museum of American History: Department of Collections Management Services; Facilities Planning & Management; Office of Exhibition Services

★ The National Museum of American History is grateful to the many organizations and individuals, both active and retired, of the U.S. Army and its contractors whose technical support,
advice, and hard work made this exhibition possible.

★ Support for this exhibition has been provided by the United States Army Center of Military History and the Army Historical Foundation with generous contributions from:
• Lockheed-Martin
• The USAA Charitable Trust
• The Carlyle Group
• Boeing
• Halliburton
• General Motors
• United Defense
• The McCormick Tribune Foundation
• BF Goodrich

★ The Museum gratefully acknowledges the following individuals, organizations, and corporations who gave their time and support to the exhibition, or lent or donated objects that appear in the exhibition:
• Alabama Department of Archives and History
• Anne S.K. Brown Military Collection, Brown University
• Appomattox Courthouse National Historical Park
• Arizona Historical Society, Tucson
• B&O Railroad Museum
• Susan D. Beller and Myron J. Liberman, in memory of Ester and Gilbert Liberman
• Estate of Gen. Wilmon W. Blackmar
• Mr. and Mrs. Albert Borkin in memory of Morris Borkin
• The Brennan Collection
• CORBIS
• Corbis/Bettmann
• Elizabeth B. Custer
• John William Christopher Draper/James Christopher Draper
• Freer Gallery of Art
• Louis Glanzman
• Julia Dent Grant
• William H. Guthman
• Historic Lexington Foundation
• History Program, National Imagery and Mapping Agency
• C. Bremer Jackson
• Library of Congress
• J. Mortimer Lichtenauer
• Little Bighorn Battlefield National Monument
• Greg E. Mathieson/United States Military Academy
• Colonel John J. McElwee, Retired
• The Honorable George B. McClellan, son of General George B. McClellan
• Montana Historical Society
• The Moorland-Spingarn Research Center, Howard University
• National Air and Space Museum
• National Museum of Natural History, Department of Anthropology
• National Archives and Records Administration
• National Gallery of Art
• National Geographic Society
• National Portrait Gallery
• NMAH Archive Center
• New York State Library
• George A. Norton
• Mrs. Bridget E. O'Farrell
• Family of General John J. Pershing
• The Robert E. Petersen Sports Afield Collection
• F. E. Robinson
• Mrs. A. S. Rowan
• Gen. H. Norman Schwarzkopf (U.S. Army, retired)
• Smithsonian Archives
• Smithsonian Institution Libraries
• Stratford Hall Plantation, Robert E. Lee Memorial Association
• Colonel Charles P. Summerall, Jr.
• The National Society of the Colonial Dames of America
• June Tuck
• U.S. Army Center of Military History
• U.S. Army Military History Institute
• U.S. Army Quartermaster Corps Museum, Ft. Lee, Virginia
• University of Missouri-Columbia
• United States Military Academy Library
• West Point Museum Collection, United States Military Academy Museum
• United States Postal Service
• Franklin Wingard
• Norman K. Wolfe, nephew of General Frank Lahm

Cadets throw hats in the air at graduation.

FOREWORD

IT BEGAN as a fortress; jutting into the Hudson River fifty miles above Manhattan in the shadows of Bear Mountain and Storm King Mountain. It was the "river and the rock" that the British desperately wanted to seize to sunder the patriots of New England from their compatriots and crush the revolution that would make America.

It became a school for soldiers who would fight our wars and build and shape our country and the world.

And, it has become something more: a symbol of selfless service to the nation by men and women of character and commitment. Generations of graduates have kept faith with the simple but profound command, "Duty, Honor, Country."

In *West Point in the Making of America,* the Smithsonian Institution celebrates the service and sacrifice of early generations of West Point graduates and their families as West Point celebrates its bicentennial. Through the lives of these men, you will see the struggles of a new nation to defend itself, to build the roads and canals that are its economic sinews, to explore and expand on a great continent, to preserve our precious Union through the trial of the Civil War, and to emerge as a world power at the beginning of the 20th century.

In this book, you will encounter West Point graduates who are renowned. But you will also meet many others who, while not well known, served with distinction and made extraordinary contributions to our country.

In this book, you will see epochal events in our history through the careers of West Pointers. There is no more pivotal and crucial event in our history than the Civil War. It was a war that divided the nation and, in a personal and traumatic way, it divided West Point. Of the war's 60 major battles, West Pointers commanded the forces on both sides in 55 of these battles. In the remaining five, they commanded one of the opposing forces. The names of graduates in Blue and Gray reverberate through our history: Ulysses S. Grant, Robert E. Lee, George McClellan, Stonewall Jackson, George Meade, James Longstreet, William Tecumseh Sherman, and the list goes on.

After four bloody years, the war ended with two West Pointers noting their assent to the terms in the parlor of Wilmer McLean's home in Appomattox Court House, Virginia. Ulysses Simpson Grant (Class of 1843) harnessed the industrial strength of the North with his own relentless determination to subdue Confederate forces, led for years from one victory to another by Robert E. Lee (Class of 1829). Fortunately for the nation, their prowess in war was matched by their mutual determination to forge a peace that could lead to reconciliation.

The decades after the Civil War saw West Pointers serving on the frontiers of America and around the world as the global presence of the United States expanded.

In this book, you will come to understand that West Point was not only our first military academy, it was our first school of engineering. At the beginning of our national and military history, technology was inextricably bound to our military readiness and our national purpose. It remains so today. And, West Point remains an arsenal of ideas and intellectual inquiry for our army and for America.

In 1902, West Point celebrated its centennial. Douglas MacArthur was a cadet in the Class of 1903. Dwight Eisenhower and Omar Bradley were school boys in the heartland of America, barely beginning lives that would lead them to graduate in the West Point Class of 1915. In the 20th century, these West Pointers and their contemporaries would profoundly shape our army, our nation, and the world.

In 2002, as West Point celebrates its bicentennial, another generation of Americans proudly forms the Long Gray Line. They too have and will assume positions as leaders of character committed to selfless service to the nation. In the words of a melody close to the hearts of all West Pointers,

> The long grey line of us stretches
> Through the years of a century told
> And the last man feels to his marrow
> The grip of your far off hold

In this extraordinary book, you too will feel the grip of West Point and the profound contributions of its graduates to our country.

Yours,

Jack Reed

United States Senator, Rhode Island, West Point, Class of 1971

TWO HUNDRED YEARS OF WEST POINT

IN MARCH 2002, the United States Military Academy at West Point, New York, celebrated 200 years of producing leaders for the United States Army—and also for American science, education, engineering, exploration, public works, business, manufacturing, communication, and transportation.

In the bicentennial exhibition to which this book is a companion, the Smithsonian Institution's National Museum of American History looks at the lives of selected West Point graduates, some famous, others less well known. All attended the Academy, most of them between 1802 and 1918. Families are also part of the story, because they helped sustain army communities. The stories of the officers and their families blend into the U.S. Army's major functions of 19th- and early 20th-century America: building the nation's infrastructure of roads, bridges, canals, and railroads; exploring its territories from the Mississippi to the Pacific; and fighting its wars—the role of the West Pointers in engineering, exploration, and war.

View of antebellum
West Point (detail)

IN TELLING THE STORY of West Point's contribution to the making of America from its founding through World War I, the National Museum of American History's West Point bicentennial exhibition relies on almost 400 images and artifacts, approximately half of which appear in this catalogue. Images and objects are set within a historical framework and 51 biographical sketches help bring the story to life. The exhibition also features three videos: an introduction narrated by Gen. H. Norman Schwarzkopf; a presentation on the Travis Panorama, a series of panels painted by William Travis that depict the career of Gen. William Starke Rosecrans and the Army of the Cumberland during the Civil War (1861–1865); and a newsreel-like view of World War I (1914–1918). In addition, the exhibition includes three interactive games on Western exploration; Civil War battles and leaders; and the contributions of West Pointers in invention, engineering, and war.

CHAPTER 1

"Two Hundred Years of West Point" introduces the United States Military Academy at West Point, following its history from its founding in 1802 through World War I. Profiled are Dennis Hart Mahan and Sylvanus Thayer, who, in the antebellum years, helped make West Point the nation's preeminent school of engineering.

CHAPTER 2

"The Antebellum Army" spotlights the work of West Pointers from the Academy's founding (1802) to the outbreak of the Civil War (1861). It covers their Western exploration, building of railroads, and wars against the Seminole Indians and Mexico. Profiled are John James Abert, George Bomford, George Brinton McClellan, William Gibbs McNeill, David Moniac, Alfred Mordecai, Samuel Ringgold, Gouvenour Kemble Warren, and George Washington Whistler.

CHAPTER 3

"Civil War and Reconstruction" considers the dilemmas of choosing sides in a civil war, and explores the roles of West Pointers in organizing the war effort, fighting the war, and reconstructing the Union. Profiled are Joseph Reid Anderson, Robert Anderson, Pierre Gustave Toutant Beauregard, Alexander Brydie Dyer, Josiah Gorgas, Ulysses Simpson Grant, Herman Haupt, Oliver Otis Howard, Thomas Jonathan "Stonewall" Jackson, Robert Edward Lee, Montgomery Cunningham Meigs, Robert Parker Parrott, John Clifford Pemberton, William Tecumseh Sherman, George Henry Thomas, and Thomas Murray Tolman.

66 Your duty here at West Point has been to fit men to do well in war. But it is a noteworthy fact that you also have fitted them to do singularly well in peace. 99

PRESIDENT THEODORE ROOSEVELT, SPEECH FOR THE WEST POINT CENTENNIAL COMMENCEMENT EXERCISES, 11 JUNE 1902

CHAPTER 4

"An Army for the Nation" surveys the period between the end of the
Civil War (1865) and the beginning of World War I (1914). It looks at
the lives of West Pointers (and their families) on western army posts,
their conduct of the Spanish-American War (1898–1899) and Philippine
War (1899–1902), and their roles in such major engineering projects
as rebuilding Washington, D.C., and completing the Panama Canal.
Profiled are Thomas Lincoln Casey, George Armstrong Custer,
George Crook, Henry Ossian Flipper, David DuBose Gaillard, George
Washington Goethals, Frank Ross McCoy, Ranald Slidell Mackenzie,
Fayette Washington Roe, and Andrew Summers Rowan.

CHAPTER 5

"America in the Great War" discusses the contributions of West Point
graduates in World War I. It shows their roles in organizing army
supply, mobilizing manpower and industry, and fighting on the Western
Front. Profiled are Enoch Herbert Crowder, William Crozier, Hugh
Samuel Johnson, Peyton Conway March, John Joseph Pershing, Hugh
Lenox Scott, Henry Granville Sharpe, George Owen Squier, and
Charles Pelot Summerall.

CHAPTER 6

"West Point in the 20th Century" sketches the changing character of
the military academy since World War I. It surveys the impact of both
world wars on West Point, examines West Pointers in World War II
(1939–1945), and suggests the changes in West Point curriculum and
admission policies that transformed the Academy in the later 20th
century. Profiled are Creighton Williams Abrams, Jr., Omar Nelson
Bradley, Garrison Holt Davidson, Benjamin Oliver Davis, Jr., Douglas
MacArthur, and the women of the Class of 1980.

When the United States Military Academy was founded in March 1802,
America was still a small emerging nation hugging the eastern seaboard.
By 1918, America spanned the continent and beyond. It had become an
industrial powerhouse and won World War I. Much of the credit for
that century of achievement lies with the graduates of West Point.

*"I recommend to your fostering care as one of our safest means of national
defense the Military Academy. This institution has already exercised the
happiest influence upon the moral and intellectual character of our army."*

PRESIDENT ANDREW JACKSON, IN HIS ANNUAL MESSAGE TO CONGRESS, 1834

WEST POINT AND ITS PEOPLE

GEORGE Washington first proposed a military academy in 1783, but critics opposed this relatively new idea of a special school to train army officers as too European. They deemed it incompatible with democratic institutions, fearing the creation of a military aristocracy. Finally, two decades after Washington's first proposal, on 16 March 1802, the United States Military Academy was founded. It stood on a commanding bluff overlooking the Hudson River at West Point, New York, fifty miles north of Manhattan.

West Point became an important American institution in the years before the Civil War, establishing itself as the country's finest school of engineering and science. Its graduates held key roles in virtually every aspect of American life. They also began to distinguish themselves as junior officers, many later rising to command armies on both sides of the Civil War. But the Academy's reputation suffered because so many graduates joined the Confederacy. It had also become only one among many other fine engineering schools.

During the later 19th century, West Point focused on a more narrowly military curriculum and its graduates formed the heart of the army's officer corps. When the United States entered World War I, West Pointers had charge of almost every major staff bureau and field command. Army and nation had combined to make the country a world power.

> **"***A Peace Establishment for the United States of America may in my opinion . . . [include] Academies, one or more for the Instruction of the Art Military; particularly those Branches of it which respect Engineering and Artillery, which are highly essential, and the knowledge of which is most difficult to obtain.***"**
>
> GEORGE WASHINGTON, "SENTIMENTS ON A PEACE ESTABLISHMENT," MAY 1783

George Washington's field, or marquee, tent, preserved since the American Revolutionary War (1775–1783)

General Washington at Princeton by Charles Peale Polk

A SCHOOL FOR THE NATION

AN uncertain mission, internal conflicts, and inadequate staff plagued the military academy's first fifteen years. That all began to change with the appointment of Sylvanus Thayer (Class of 1808) as superintendent in 1817. Following the example of the famous French engineering and artillery schools that the army had sent him to study, Thayer made West Point America's national engineering school. West Point combined officer training with a highly technical undergraduate education. All cadets took the same classes; striking the right balance has remained a constant subject of discussion among the faculty.

Engineering itself became the army's elite branch of service, the first choice by those who ranked highest in a graduating class. Lower rank-ing cadets went to the cavalry, infantry, and other branches. West Point also became the nation's major source of civil engineers and of engi-neering educators. In the three decades before the Civil War, West Pointers as teachers, writers, and practitioners fostered science and engineering at Cornell, Harvard, Yale, and other colleges. They also helped staff the other service academies that later opened: the U.S. Naval Academy at Annapolis, Maryland, in 1845 and the U.S. Air Force Academy at Colorado Springs, Colorado, in 1959.

> **❝***It is important our officers should gain a knowledge of the European Military Establishments, their fortifications, Mil'y Schools & Military Work Shops; to those objects I presume the enquiries of ...Capt. Thayer would be diverted, & also to the collection of rare books, maps, plans and instruments for the Military Academy.* **❞**
>
> BRIG. GEN. JOSEPH G. SWIFT TO SECRETARY OF WAR JAMES MONROE, APRIL 1815

Cadet Life at West Point, sketched by Theodore R. Davis in *Harper's Weekly,* 4 July 1868

SYLVANUS THAYER

1785–1872   Class of 1808

Thayer had already graduated from Dartmouth College before attending West Point. Commissioned in the Corps of Engineers, he worked on coastal fortifications in New York and New England. He served as a staff officer in the War of 1812 1812–1815), rising from second lieutenant to major.

After the war, Thayer embarked on a two-year inspection tour of European military schools and installations, returning in 1817 to become superintendent at West Point. The educational and administrative reforms he initiated during his sixteen-year tenure created a preeminent school of engineering, making him remembered ever after as "the father of the Military Academy."

Thayer resigned as superintendent in 1833 but remained an army engineer, working on harbor improvements in New England. He retired in 1863 with the rank of brigadier general. In 1867 the lifelong bachelor endowed the Thayer School of Engineering at Dartmouth College and designed the new school's curriculum.

DENNIS HART MAHAN

1802–1871   Class of 1824

As an undergraduate at West Point, Mahan taught mathematics to underclassmen. Graduating at the top of his class, he soon returned to the Academy, remaining on the faculty for more than forty years.

Teaching mathematics, and later a professor of engineering, Mahan redesigned the Academy's engineering programs. His textbooks became American standards of engineering instruction.

Mahan also taught the course on military science taken by virtually every West Pointer who fought in the Civil War. Despite its odd title, his textbook, *Elementary Treatise on Advance-Guard, Out-Post, and Detachment Service of Troops* (1847, often reprinted), was America's first comprehensive work on tactics and strategy.

Professor and Mrs. Mahan, the former Mary Helena Okill, raised five children. Their oldest son, Alfred Thayer, chose the U.S. Naval Academy and became a renowned naval strategist and historian. A younger son, Frederick August, graduated from West Point in 1867.

"*By rapidity of movement we can, like the Romans, make war feed war.*"

DENNIS HART MAHAN, *ELEMENTARY TREATISE ON ADVANCE-GUARD, OUT-POST, AND DETACHMENT SERVICE OF TROOPS*, 1847

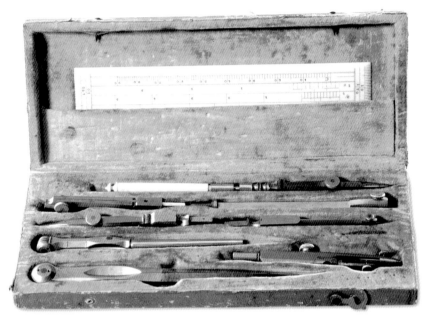

Every cadet was issued a set of drawing instruments. This set belonged to Cadet George Brinton McClellan (Class of 1846).

The Crozet protractor is named after its designer, Claude Crozet, a mathematics teacher at West Point from 1817 to 1823.

This magnifying glass on a stand was standard equipment in the West Point laboratory before the Civil War.

A DIVISION of HORSE ARTILLERY at FULL SPEED.

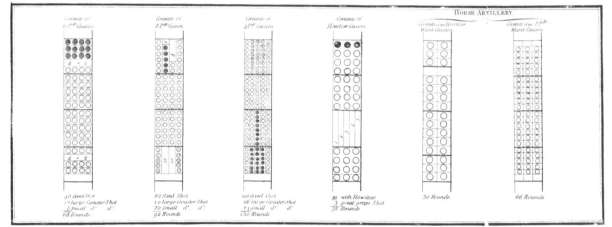

Louis de Tousard's *American Artillerist's Companion; or, Elements of Artillery* (three volumes; 1809–1813) was the first American publication on its subject. This plate from volume three shows horse artillery in action and various types of shot arranged in caissons (artillery supply wagons).

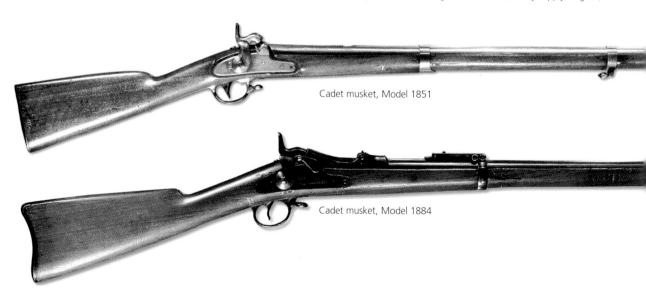

Cadet musket, Model 1851

Cadet musket, Model 1884

Drawing was an important part of cadet training. In addition to its relevance to engineering and map-making, it helped cadets learn how to reproduce on paper what they observed in the field. Above is a rendering of a gun by Herbert S. Whipple (Class of 1885).

Cadet Room, 1842, drawn by Cadet George H. Derby (Class of 1846)

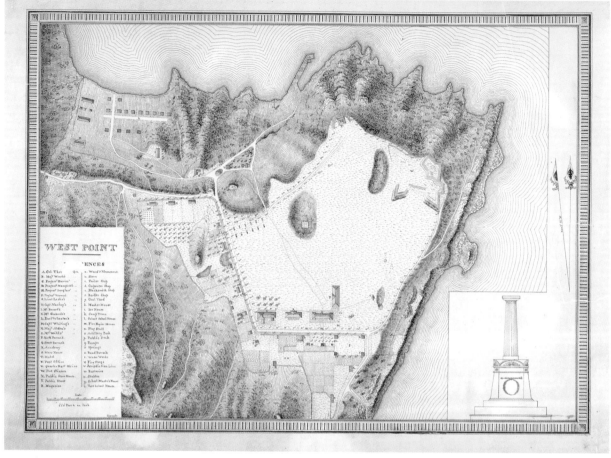

Map of West Point drawn by Cadet Thomas Swords, about 1825

Illustration by Cadet James A. McNeill Whistler for "United States Military Academy, Song of the Graduates, 1852." Whistler never graduated from West Point and later became a world-famous artist.

WEST POINT AFTER THE CIVIL WAR

AFTER the Civil War, West Point was but one engineering school among many. A number of other centers of engineer training, many shaped by West Pointers, had sprung up before the war. Yet West Point remained a fine engineering school and its graduates continued to make their presence felt, overseeing the construction of such Washington landmarks as the Washington Monument and the Library of Congress. They also contributed mightily to one of the age's great engineering projects, the Panama Canal.

Cadets in summer encampment, 1905

But technical military proficiency increasingly became the focus of
studies at West Point. Its graduates led the army's professionalization,
the expansion of military higher education, and the creation of a
general staff. When the United States entered World War I, West
Pointers took charge of virtually every aspect of mobilization,
logistics, and combat.

Cadet mess, Grant Hall, 1896

Harper's Weekly

HAZING AT THE WEST POINT MILITARY ACADEMY

"Hazing the Plebes," from *Harper's Weekly*, 1902. Upperclassmen regularly subjected new cadets, or plebes (for plebeian), to teasing or harassment as a means of ushering them into their new army life. Periodically, however, such hazing degenerated into brutality or even violence, despite the best effort of superintendents and faculty to keep it under control. In 1900 Cadet Oscar L. Booz resigned from West Point after becoming the subject of particularly vicious hazing. His much-publicized death in 1901, which his family attributed to the hazing, prompted a congressional investigation and anti-hazing legislation.

HARPER'S WEEKLY.

THE CAVALRY SCHOOL, AT WEST POINT.—Drawn by R. F. Zogbaum.—[See Page 358.]

Cavalry training in the old riding hall, as depicted in a drawing by R. F. Zogbaum in *Harper's Weekly*

2

THE ANTEBELLUM ARMY

NOT EVERYONE who went to West Point before the Civil War remained in the army, but those who did played key roles in the eastern Indian wars and the War with Mexico (1846–1848). They also helped explore the new lands west of the Mississippi and build the nation's roads.

West Pointers led many of the expeditions westward, explorations part military reconnaissance, part scientific inquiry, part treasure hunt. They surveyed and mapped the land, gathered information, identified potentially valuable resources, collected specimens, and wrote reports. The military posts they established often became the nucleus of towns and cities.

Whether as army officers or civilian engineers, West Pointers built America's roads and canals, bridges and railroads. They also transplanted major features of military organization to the new railroad corporations and pioneered mass production. In these activities and others, West Pointers helped lay the groundwork for America's economic development, intellectual growth, and territorial expansion-engineering, exploration, and war.

U.S. forces at Churubusco in August 1847, as depicted by James Walker in one of his series of nine Mexican War paintings (detail)

THE WESTERN RECONNAISSANCE

T HE U.S. Army played a key role in exploring the nation's vast new lands acquired through purchase (such as Louisiana and the watersheds of the Mississippi and Missouri Rivers, 1803) and conquest (such as California and the Southwest, 1848) during the first half of the 19th century. Military-scientific expeditions crisscrossed the West, mapping the country, gathering scientific data, identifying potential resources for exploitation, and surveying routes for roads and railroads.

Through the 1850s, this reconnaissance was led by the army's topographical engineers, or topogs as they were often called, most of them graduates of West Point. Unlike the regular army engineers who worked mainly on construction and fortification, the topogs specialized in mapping and surveying. Their skills and hard work opened lands formerly known only to native inhabitants and a relatively small number of fur trappers and traders to economic exploitation and a growing influx of settlers from the eastern United States and from Europe.

Upper Cataract Creek Near Big Canyon, 1864, by J.J. Young from a sketch by F.W. Egloffstein

66 *. . . our manifest destiny to overspread the continent allotted by Providence for the free development of our yearly multiplying millions.* **99**

EDITOR JOHN L. O'SULLIVAN, *DEMOCRATIC REVIEW*, JULY–AUGUST 1845

Dress uniform of a topographical engineer

JOHN JAMES ABERT

1788–1863   Class of 1811

Abert's name is almost synonymous with the army's Corps of Topographical Engineers, which he headed for thirty-two years. He left the army upon graduation from West Point and the next year married Ellen Matlack Stretch, who often accompanied him in his later travels. One of their six children followed their father to West Point, James William (Class of 1842).

The War of 1812 brought Abert back to the army in 1814 as a topographical engineer, and fifteen years later he headed the corps. Under his leadership, the corps' thirty-six officers, most of them also West Pointers, furthered American science with data from their western expeditions. They also helped turn a relatively unknown wilderness west of the Mississippi into an extensively surveyed, well-mapped, built up, interconnected, and increasingly settled landscape. Abert retired in 1861 and the corps itself was abolished in 1863, mission accomplished.

> *[The topographic engineers are] the eyes of the commanding general...With these he can see the country, and can know how to direct and combine all movements or marches...without them he is literally groping in the dark.*
>
> J.J. ABERT, *ANNUAL REPORT 1848*

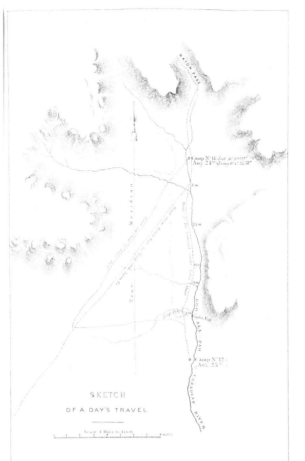

Lt. James William Abert, Col. Abert's son, sketched the route of a day's travel during his 1845 reconnaissance of the southwestern United States.

This engraving, *La Ciudad de Santa Fe*, appeared in Lt. James William Abert's (Class of 1842) report of his 1846–1847 New Mexico expedition. Lt. Abert was Col. Abert's son.

GOUVENOUR KEMBLE WARREN

1830–1882   Class of 1850

Assigned to the topographical engineers after graduation, Warren participated in surveys of the Mississippi Delta and railroad routes to the Pacific. He later compiled the first accurate map of the trans-Mississippi West.

A lifelong champion of Indian rights, Warren in the mid-1850s amassed an important collection of Sioux and other northern Plains Indian material culture. Passed to the fledgling Smithsonian Institution, it joined the stream of specimens and notes from western exploration upon which such sciences as natural history, geology, and ethnology flourished in America.

The Civil War made Warren a major general. In 1863 he married Emily Forbes Chase (they would have two children). Just two weeks later, he spotted the Gettysburg battlefield's key ground feature in time for its seizure by Union forces. Today his statue stands on Little Round Top, overlooking the battlefield his topographical eye helped to win.

> **"***I have always found the Dakotas [Sioux] exceedingly reasonable beings, with a very proper appreciation of what are their own rights.***"**

GOUVENOUR K. WARREN, *PRELIMINARY REPORT OF EXPLORATIONS IN NEBRASKA AND DAKOTA*, 1858

Compiled from every available source, Gouvenour Warren's 1859 map was
the first accurate depiction of the entire United States west of the Mississippi.

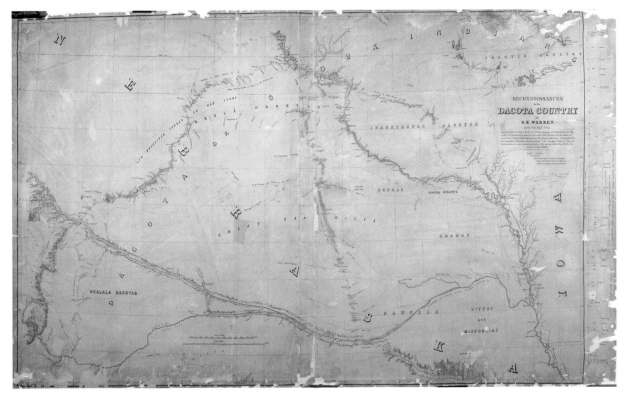

Lt. Warren's *Reconnaissances in the Dacota Country*, from an 1855 expedition

The report by William Hemsley Emory (Class of 1831) of his 1846 expedition from Fort Leavenworth, Missouri, to San Diego, California, published in 1848, included this drawing of a beaded lizard.

WARS OF EXPANSION

THE army was pivotal to American expansion before the Civil War. West Point graduates, still few in number, played only a limited role in the War of 1812. The continuing Indian wars—ignited by settlers flooding into the newly opened lands between the Allegheny Mountains and the Mississippi during the first half of the 19th century—were another story.

In conflicts with Native Americans from the Creek War (1811–1814) to the Second Seminole War (1835–1842), West Point gave the regular army most of its junior officers. Many young officers received their first taste of combat in small unit actions against highly elusive foes.

The War with Mexico was fought more conventionally, but no less successfully, adding large new territories to the growing republic. Most of the young officers who distinguished themselves against Mexican forces were graduates of West Point, but their commanders were politically appointed. Little more than a decade later, many of these young officers themselves commanded armies in the Civil War.

> **❝**..*the War between the United States and Mexico might ... have lasted some four or five years, within its first half, more defeats than victories falling to our share, whereas in less than two campaigns we conquered a great country and a peace without the loss of a single battle or skirmish..***❞**

WINFIELD SCOTT, IN *REPORT OF THE COMMISSION ... TO EXAMINE INTO THE ORGANIZATION, SYSTEM OF DISCIPLINE, AND COURSE OF INSTRUCTION OF THE UNITED STATES MILITARY ACADEMY AT WEST POINT, 1860*

ARRIVAL OF

THE. S^o. C^a. DRAGOONS AT THE WITHLACOOCHE

"Arrival of the So. Ca. [3rd] Dragoons at the Withlacooche [River, Florida]"

SAMUEL RINGGOLD

1800–1846 × Class of 1818

For twenty years after West Point, Ringgold's military career gave little hint of special distinction. But in 1838 he received orders to create the U.S. Army's first "horse artillery" battery. Horses had always pulled the guns and caissons (ammunition wagons), but in this new formation, gunners rode their own horses.

Ringgold's battery comprised six guns, each followed by twelve mounted gunners, plus caissons and other gear. Drilled to near perfection, they took only minutes to gallop up, unlimber their guns, fire, remount, and gallop to a new position, a show so impressive the army used it for recruiting.

Ringgold proved that his battery was not just for show during the Mexican War, at the Battle of Palo Alto (1846). His guns almost single-handedly repulsed repeated Mexican attacks. In the moment of triumph, Ringgold fell to a Mexican cannon ball, becoming the first American killed in the Mexican War and the war's first hero.

> **"***During the night he gave many incidents of the battle, and spoke with much pride of the execution of his shot.***"**

DEATHBED CONVERSATION OF SAMUEL RINGGOLD, AS REPORTED BY THE NAVAL PHYSICIAN IN ATTENDANCE, 8–11 MAY 1846

DAVID MONIAC

1802–1836 · Class of 1822

Silhouette of David Moniac. There is no known image of him.

> **"** *He was ...cordially esteemed by all who knew him. There was really nothing in his quiet life to distinguish him from the majority of the country gentlemen of his time & day.* **"**

DAVID MONIAC, AS REMEMBERED BY HIS KINSMAN, TOM TATE TUNSTALL

Although often called West Point's first Indian graduate, Moniac, like many Americans, was of mixed heritage—not only Creek, but also Dutch, Scottish, and English. He resigned his commission soon after graduation, returning to his Alabama home and marrying Mary Powell, cousin to Osceola (Billy Powell), later a Florida Seminole leader. The couple had a son and a daughter.

Little is known of Moniac during the years before his return to military service. Apparently he was a cotton planter, slave holder, and breeder of race horses. In 1836, Moniac was appointed captain of Creek mounted volunteers in the Second Seminole War. Fought in Florida, this was the last major war pitting the U.S. Army against Indians east of the Mississippi. On 21 November 1836, less than a week after his promotion to major, he died leading a charge at the Battle of Wahoo Swamp.

ASEOLA,

A SEMINOLE LEADER.

Troops fording Lake Ocklawaha

Seminole Indians attacked the fort at Lake Okeechobee on 25 December 1837.

A longtime opponent of white encroachment on Indian lands, the Seminole chieftain Osceola (about 1800–1838) led his people into the Second Seminole War.

GEORGE BRINTON McCLELLAN

1828–1885 ★ Class of 1846

McClellan graduated from West Point into the Mexican War, serving as a combat engineer, and three times cited for his zeal and bravery under fire. He then taught at West Point, surveyed transcontinental railroad routes, studied European military organization, and designed the army's standard saddle.

McClellan resigned his commission in 1857 to become a railroad executive. In 1860 he married Ellen Marcy, the daughter of Randolph B. Marcy (Class of 1832). During the Civil War, Marcy became his son-in-law's chief of staff.

Back in uniform when war began, McClellan led a bold, victorious western Virginia campaign that won him fame and command of Union forces. But that boldness and victory now deserted him, although he proved an efficient organizer well liked by his men. Removed from command, he turned to politics, failing in an 1864 bid for the presidency but later winning two terms as governor of New Jersey.

"*Hip! Hip! Hurray! War at last sure enough! Aint it glorious!*"

GEORGE B. McCLELLAN TO HIS SISTER, 13 MAY 1846

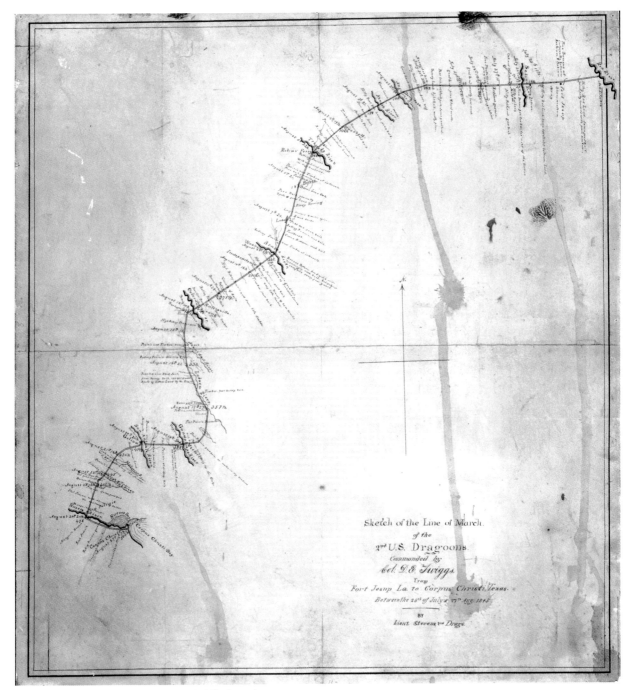

In 1845, the 2nd Dragoons marched through difficult terrain
from Fort Jesup, Louisiana, to Corpus Christi, Texas, 503 miles
in thirty-one days along the line shown.

ENGINEERING FOR A NEW NATION

WEST Point long remained America's only engineering school, and it more than held its own against competition from other schools before the Civil War. It always trained military engineers, but the same course of study also helped meet America's expanding demand for civil engineering. West Point graduates helped survey and construct the nation's roads, canals, and utilities. They devised new techniques in iron-working and chemical manufacturing. They helped pioneer the development of interchangeable parts manufacturing, called the American system, which astonished Europe at the Great Exhibition of 1851 in London.

As leaders in early railroad building, West Point graduates applied their military training to the management of the new kind of business corporations that railroads pioneered. Two of the four-member engineering team hired by America's first major railroad, the Baltimore & Ohio, and nine of the ten topographical assistants were West Pointers. Most of these assistants became railroad engineers, forming the core of this new profession.

> **❝** *Several able and efficient members of the Topographical Corps have been detailed in service of the company.* **❞**
>
> ANNUAL REPORT, BALTIMORE & OHIO RAILROAD CO., 1 OCTOBER 1827

The Thomas Viaduct carried the Baltimore & Ohio Railroad across the Patapsco River, as shown in an 1835 lithograph by Thomas Campbell.

GEORGE BOMFORD

1782–1848   Class of 1805

After graduating from West Point, Bomford continued his army career in the Corps of Engineers, building seacoast fortifications. He also experimented with designs for heavy guns able to fire both explosive shells and solid shot.

When the War of 1812 began, Bomford moved to the new Army Ordnance Department. It was created to replace a loosely supervised group of private suppliers as the army's primary source for artillery, firearms, and ammunition. The new department also took charge of the nation's arsenals, even then developing the uniformity system of interchangeable parts manufacturing.

First as assistant chief of ordnance, then chief from 1821 to 1842, Bomford promoted the use of the uniformity system to manufacturing small arms. He also attempted to standardize the army's field artillery.

Saddle used by George B. McClellan

Interchangeability required parts made to very precise measurements. Gauges such as this lock receiving gauge (with lock) and a trigger guard and receiver gauge (with trigger guard) helped provide such precision. They were key elements of the American system of interchangeable parts manufacturing pioneered in army arsenals.

The rifled musket, Model 1842, was a product of the American system of interchangeable parts manufacturing. It became the U.S. Army's first standard-issue firearm with interchangeable parts.

WILLIAM GIBBS M^CNEILL

1801–1853   Class of 1817

GEORGE WASHINGTON WHISTLER

1800–1849   Class of 1819

McNeill (above) and Whistler (below) began their lifelong friendship as cadets. After his first wife, Mary Smith, died very young, Whistler married McNeill's sister, Anna Matilda. Their son, the noted painter James McNeill Whistler, attended West Point without graduating.

Both McNeill and Whistler spent their active army careers as topographical engineers. During the 1820s, when West Point graduates were virtually America's only trained engineers, the government began lending their services to private companies. McNeill and Whistler went to the Baltimore & Ohio Railroad. Other railroad and related engineering projects followed, both before and after they resigned their commissions, Whistler in 1833, McNeill in 1837. Whistler went to Russia in 1842 to supervise construction of the Moscow–St. Petersburg railroad, Russia's first. Other projects followed, and he never returned.

ALFRED MORDECAI

1804–1887 • Class of 1823

Mordecai led his class academically and taught engineering at West Point for two years. In 1832 he shifted to the Ordnance Corps, in which he pioneered the application of scientific methods to developing and testing weapons and ammunition. He also played major roles in compiling the army's first ordnance manual (1841) and reorganizing army artillery along more rational lines (1849).

In 1861 Mordecai, a North Carolinian, resigned his commission, refusing to break his oath but unwilling to fight against southern family and friends. He spent the war years teaching mathematics in Philadelphia, near the family of his wife, Sara Ann Hays Mordecai. Their son Alfred graduated from West Point in 1861 and fought for the Union. After the war, Mordecai turned to railroading, briefly as an engineer in Mexico, then as an official with the Pennsylvania Railroad.

The great advantages that will attend this extreme simplification of field artillery must be obvious to every one who reflects on the inconveniences of the present complex system.

ALFRED MORDECAI, *MILITARY COMMISSION TO EUROPE IN 1855 AND 1856*, 1860

In 1834, Andrew Talcott, an engineer, surveyor, and astronomer, invented the zenith telescope. It used astronomical sightings to determine latitude more precisely. The result greatly improved mapping of previously uncharted territory.

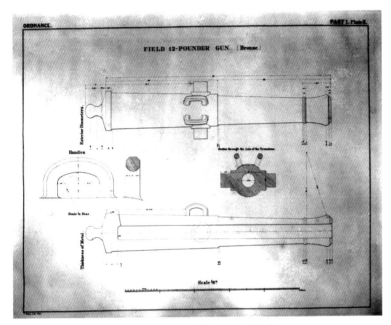

Field twelve-pounder gun (bronze). Part One, Plate Two in Alfred Mordecai, *Artillery for the Land Service of the United States* (1849)

Model of a bridge using all-wood trusses, a construction method devised by Stephen H. Long, onetime West Point instructor and topographical engineer

3

CIVIL WAR AND RECONSTRUCTION

TENSIONS BETWEEN North and South over slavery and states' rights erupted into war in 1861. Although the Union enjoyed far greater resources, it also faced the harder and more costly task of waging offensive war to conquer the Confederacy. Secession required the South only to stand on the defensive to stave off Northern attempts at reunification. West Point graduates commanded forces both North and South.

The training they shared had not prepared them for the immense changes in military technology and industry during the middle third of the 19th century that greatly affected the course of the war. Abundant rifled firearms dramatically transformed land combat, while steam power revolutionized the production and distribution of supplies. Both sides struggled to adapt to these dramatic changes.

By 1865 the United States may have been the strongest military power in the world. But the great citizen armies of the Civil War were rapidly demobilized, leaving only the small regular army to support the reconstruction of the conquered South.

The first panel of thirty-three painted by William De Laney Trimble Travis shortly after the Civil War (detail). It depicts a young soldier in the Federal Army of the Cumberland bidding farewell to home and family.

ORGANIZING FOR WAR

THE Civil War straddled two ages. It was both the last great preindustrial war and the first major war of the industrial era. For the North, the central problem was bringing to the battlefield its immense superiority in manpower, agriculture, industry, and transportation. The South's critical problem was creating an industrial base for war-making.

By the time of the Civil War, American industrialization and the expansion of communications with railroad and telegraph made logistics—obtaining and distributing war supplies—even more important than in earlier wars. No longer could armies so readily live off the land and obtain their supplies from local sources.

Neither side was well prepared for war and no one fully anticipated the full scope of what was to come. Organizing the war effort began as a makeshift process that only gradually assumed rational form. West Pointers played key roles for North and South. Two stand out for their extraordinary achievement: Confederate Chief of Ordnance Josiah Gorgas (Class of 1841) and Union Quartermaster-General Montgomery C. Meigs (Class of 1836).

> **"***That man Haupt has built a bridge across Potomac Creek, about 400 feet long and nearly 100 feet high, over which loaded trains are running every hour; and, upon my word, gentlemen, there is nothing in it but beanpoles and corn stalks.***"**
>
> ABRAHAM LINCOLN, 23 MAY 1862

Herman Haupt supervises construction of a military railroad in Virginia, 1863. The first U.S. railroad in the modern sense—a steam locomotive on tracks pulling a train of cars carrying passengers and freight—began operations in 1830. Three decades later, on the eve of the Civil War, 30,000 miles of track tied the nation together, but the Confederacy claimed less than a third of the total. This proved of inestimable value to the North, which could far more quickly and efficiently reinforce, reequip, and resupply its armies.

HERMAN HAUPT

1817–1905   Class of 1835

Haupt resigned his commission a month after graduation to become a successful civil and railroad engineer. In 1838 he married Ann Cecilia Keller of Gettysburg, Pennsylvania. One of their eleven children also graduated from West Point.

Haupt's experience as a railroad engineer brought him back to the army in the Civil War. The railroad transportation corps he organized and trained for the Army of the Potomac became a byword for speedy and efficient construction, repair, and operation of military railroads. Haupt resigned after the Battle of Gettysburg, but the men he trained continued to supply Union armies by rail.

A half century later, war planners drew upon Haupt's Civil War experience to reorganize the domestic railroad system when it threatened to break down during World War I.

Taken in 1866, just after the Civil War ended, this official quartermaster photo depicts an infantry private dressed to march.

During the Civil War, the quartermaster issued new equipment and uniforms to foot soldiers, shown here. The four-button sack coat and forage cap (or kepi) were especially popular.

MONTGOMERY CUNNINGHAM MEIGS

1816–1892 ★ Class of 1836

As a young engineer officer after West Point, Meigs worked mainly on fortifications. In 1841 he married Louisa Rodgers. One of their four children, John, also graduated from West Point (Class of 1863), only to die in action a year later.

Meigs's career took a decisive turn when he came to Washington, D.C., in 1852. Still a first lieutenant, he received two remarkable assignments: building the Washington Aqueduct and overseeing the addition of wings and a new dome to the U.S. Capitol. Both were accomplished in fine style.

But his greatest achievements came during the Civil War. Named the army's quartermaster general, he took charge of acquiring and supplying to the Union army the food, fuel, clothing, and all the other needs of a fighting force. Largely thanks to him, the Union ultimately fielded the best-supplied army in history to that date.

Montgomery Meigs designed the Washington Aqueduct.

It is hard enough to get necessities to the troops without giving space to their candies, pies, soft drinks, and gee-gaws.

MONTGOMERY CUNNINGHAM MEIGS TO SECRETARY OF WAR EDWIN STANTON, 1864

ALEXANDER BRYDIE DYER

1815–1874 · Class of 1837

After graduating from West Point, Dyer fash-
ioned his military career in ordnance, serving
primarily in arsenals throughout the country.
In 1840 he and Elizabeth Breenshea married.
One of their six children, Alexander Jr.,
followed his father to West Point (Class of
1873). The Mexican War interrupted Dyer's
arsenal service. Fighting in Nueva Mexico,
he was twice cited for gallantry.

In 1861 Dyer, a native Virginian, stayed with
the Union. Commanding the Springfield
Armory, he oversaw a fourfold increase in
rifle production, to 1,000 per day.

Dyer declined an offer to become the army's
chief of ordnance in 1862 out of respect for
the incumbent, James W. Ripley (Class of
1814). When Ripley retired in 1864, Dyer
accepted promotion. As adept at managing
the War Department Ordnance Bureau as he
was in commanding an armory, he held the
position until his death.

> **❝***The experience of the war has shown that the breech-loading arms are
> greatly superior to muzzleloaders for infantry as well as for cavalry.***❞**

A.B. DYER TO THE SECRETARY OF WAR, 5 DECEMBER 1864

The Tredegar Iron Works in Richmond, Virginia, provided most of the South's heavy artillery and armor for the ironclad boats that challenged the Federal blockade.

Terrific combat between ironclad vessels, as the two guns of the Union ship *Monitor* confront the ten guns of the Confederate ship *Merrimack*, 1862

JOSIAH GORGAS

1818–1883   Class of 1841

Gorgas began his career as an ordnance officer at Watervliet Arsenal near Troy, New York, before touring European arsenals in 1845–1846. During the Mexican War, he commanded the Veracruz ordnance depot. Routine duties over the next thirteen years took him to arsenals in Detroit, New York, Pittsburgh and to Virginia's Fort Monroe.

While stationed at Mount Vernon Arsenal near Mobile, Alabama, Gorgas met and, in 1853, married Amelia Gayle. Although a Pennsylvanian, he followed his wife into secession.

As chief of ordnance for the Confederacy, Gorgas built an extraordinary system of acquisition, manufacture, and distribution of arms and ammunition. Largely thanks to him, Confederate troops never lacked weapons, though often short of everything else. After the war, he joined the new University of the South in Tennessee, and later became president of the University of Alabama.

CHOOSING SIDES

ALTHOUGH elected president in November 1860, Abraham Lincoln did not take office until March 1861. During the interim, South Carolina seceded from the Union, soon followed by other states of the lower South—Mississippi; Florida; Alabama; Georgia; Louisiana; and Texas.

South Carolina demanded the evacuation of Fort Sumter in Charleston Harbor. Lincoln refused and sent fresh supplies. Before they arrived, Confederate batteries ringing the harbor began shelling the fort, which soon surrendered. Lincoln called for volunteers, provoking the secession of Virginia; Arkansas; Tennessee; and North Carolina.

Choosing sides in the Civil War was an agonizing decision for many West Point graduates. Most remained loyal to their home states. Of 977 graduates of the classes of 1833 to 1861 alive when war began, 259 joined the Confederacy (including 32 Northerners), while 638 fought for the Union (including 39 Southerners).

> *❝ . . . there is no doubt bitter feeling against all 'rebels,' and I do not look for good feeling from northern friends or relatives. ❞*

ENTRY FOR 13 APRIL 1868, IN *THE JOURNALS OF JOSIAH GORGAS 1857-1878*

The Civil War began when Confederate batteries shelled Fort Sumter. The Union commander, Maj. Robert Anderson (Class of 1825), had taught the artillery course at West Point when Brig. Gen. P. G. T. Beauregard (Class of 1838), commander of the attacking Confederate forces, was a cadet.

CIVIL WAR LEADERS

THE Civil War commanders shown here, all West Point graduates, are Union generals Buell, Burnside, Grant, Hooker, McClellan, McDowell, Meade, Parke, Pope, Porter, Rosecrans, Schofield, Sheridan, Sherman, Thomas, and Warren; and Confederate commanders Beauregard, Bragg, Buckner, Hood, Jackson, A. S. Johnston, J. E. Johnston, Lee, Longstreet, Pemberton, Pickett, and Van Dorn.

P. G. T. Beauregard

B. Bragg

D. C. Buell

S. B. Buckner

A. E. Burnside

U.S. Grant

J. B. Hood

J. Hooker

T. J. Jackson

A. S. Johnston

J. E. Johnston

R. E. Lee

J. H. Longstreet

G. B. McClellan

I. McDowell

G. G. Meade

J. G. Parke

J. C. Pemberton

G. E. Pickett

J. Pope

F. J. Porter

W. S. Rosecrans

J. M. Schofield

P. H. Sheridan

W. T. Sherman

G. H. Thomas

E. Van Dorn

G. K. Warren

ROBERT ANDERSON

1805–1871 · Class of 1825

Kentucky-born of a prominent Virginia family and sympathetic to the institution of slavery, Anderson nonetheless honored his oath to United States.

Commissioned in the artillery after West Point, he served in the Second Seminole and Mexican Wars. In 1860, now a major, Anderson received a delicate assignment: commanding the Federal forts in Charleston Harbor, South Carolina. Conciliatory in his dealing with city authorities, he still refused to surrender Fort Sumter, South Carolina, until Confederate bombardment reduced the fort to ruins.

Anderson's defiance of secessionist demands and his insistence on marching out with colors flying made him one of the first Union heroes of the Civil War. Forced by ill health to retire in 1863, he briefly returned to service in 1865 to raise the U.S. flag over recaptured Fort Sumter.

"*Having defended Fort Sumter...until the quarters were entirely burned, the main gate destroyed by fire...the magazine surrounded by flame, ...I accepted the terms of evacuation offered...and marched out of Fort Sumter...with colors flying and drums beating.*"

ROBERT ANDERSON, *REPORT TO THE SECRETARY OF WAR,* 1861

JOHN CLIFFORD PEMBERTON

1814–1881   Class of 1837

Gen. John Clifford Pemberton

Martha Thompson Pemberton

Despite a Quaker upbringing in Philadelphia, Pemberton became a career soldier after West Point. His service included the Second Seminole War; the Mexican War; the Kansas border disturbances; and the Mormon War in Utah.

After returning from Mexico, Pemberton married Martha Thompson from Norfolk, Virginia. Devoted to his wife and also a strong believer in states' rights, he resigned his U.S. Army commission to join the Confederacy in 1861. Two of his brothers fought for the Union.

Questions about his loyalty to the South plagued Pemberton throughout the war, especially when he surrendered Vicksburg, Mississippi, and 27,000 troops in 1863. He returned to the Confederacy in an 1864 prisoner-of-war exchange. Ashamed of his defeat, he resigned as general and enlisted as a private. Jefferson Davis restored him to lieutenant colonel and assigned him to Richmond, Virginia. When the war ended, Pemberton retired to a Virginia farm.

PIERRE GUSTAVE TOUTANT BEAUREGARD

1815–1893 ★ Class of 1838

Beauregard chose the Corps of Engineers after graduating West Point, serving first in his home state, Louisiana, then as a staff officer during the Mexican War. Appointed West Point superintendent in 1861, he remained just five days before removal for his outspoken Southern sympathies. He soon resigned his commission to join the Confederate Army.

As commander of Confederate forces in Charleston, South Carolina, Beauregard launched the attack on Fort Sumter that triggered the Civil War. He and Confederate President Jefferson Davis (Class of 1828) were often at odds. Within months, he became more administrator than combat leader.

After the war, Beauregard returned to New Orleans to head the New Orleans, Jackson & Mississippi Railway. He later served as the city's commissioner of public works.

> **❝** *A reckless and unprincipled tyrant has invaded your soil.* **❞**

P.G.T. BEAUREGARD, *PROCLAMATION TO THE PEOPLE OF VIRGINIA*, 1 JUNE 1861

P.G.T. Beauregard commanded the Confederate army at the first major battle of the Civil War, Manassas, 21 July 1861. The South prevailed, but the army was too con- fused and exhuasted to follow up on its victory. During the battle, Beauregard noted that similarity between the Confederate "Stars and Bars," pictured here, and the U.S. flag contributed to the confusion. *Battle of Bull Run*, by Kurz and Allison, 1889.

GEORGE HENRY THOMAS

1816–1870 ★ Class of 1840

Commissioned first in the artillery, Thomas was rewarded for bravery in the Seminole War and in the Mexican War. In 1855 he joined the newly organized 2nd Cavalry regiment, a breeding ground of Confederate generals—Albert Sidney Johnston (Class of 1826), Robert E. Lee (Class of 1829), William J. Hardee (Class of 1838), Earl Van Dorn (Class of 1842), John Bell Hood (Class of 1853), and Fitzhugh Lee (Class of 1856).

Thomas, too, became a general, but in the Union army. Nicknamed "Rock of Chickamauga" for his heroic stand amid the wreckage of a defeated Union army in 1863, he won one of the great Union victories of the war in 1864, shattering the last Confederate army in the West at the Battle of Nashville.

Loyalty to the Union had its costs. Thomas's sisters in Virginia turned his picture to the wall and never spoke to him again.

“I will surrender my command without a murmur, if they wish it; but I will not act against my judgment when I know I am right.”

GEORGE HENRY THOMAS ON THE EVE OF THE BATTLE OF NASHVILLE, AS REPORTED BY JAMES H. WILSON, HIS CAVALRY COMMANDER, IN *BATTLES AND LEADERS OF THE CIVIL WAR*, 1888

The command wagon of George Henry Thomas, 1864

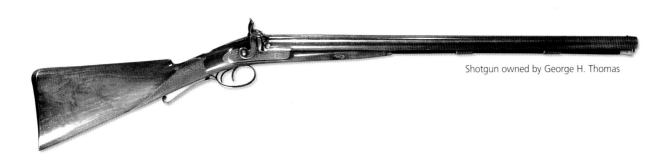

Shotgun owned by George H. Thomas

FIGHTING THE CIVIL WAR

TWO fundamental technical factors shaped Civil War fighting— rifles and railroads. Defending infantry armed with rifles and protected by breastworks or trenches exacted terrible costs from forces attacking across open ground. Counterattacks were equally costly. Railroads, which became indispensable in supplying Civil War armies, also provided defensive advantage. An advancing army moved further from its rail-supplied depots, while a defeated army fell back toward its depots and fresh supplies.

The costliness of attacks and the often inconclusive results of battle made for a long war. The Union's two decisive victories, at Vicksburg and Gettysburg in July 1863, did not end the war but marked only its halfway point.

Nothing in a West Point education had prepared officers for the new realities of rifles and railroads, and not one graduate had ever commanded an army in battle before 1861. Yet the Civil War became a West Pointers' war, with 151 Confederate and 294 Union generals. West Pointers commanded both sides in 55 of the war's 60 major battles, and one side in the other five.

> **❝***The war now is away back in the past and you [the Civil War veterans in the crowd] can tell what books can not. . . . There is many a boy here to-day who looks on war as all glory, but, boys, it is all hell.***❞**
>
> GEN. WILLIAM TECUMSEH SHERMAN, IMPROMPTU ADDRESS AT A POLITICAL RALLY IN COLUMBUS, OHIO, 11 AUGUST 1880

Union trenches before Petersburg, Virginia, 1864

The aftermath of battle

ROBERT PARKER PARROTT

1804–1877   Class of 1824

Parrott received an artillery commission upon graduation, but spent his first five years after graduation teaching physics at West Point. Promoted to captain in 1836, he was assigned as inspector of ordnance at the new West Point Foundry, a civilian enterprise. Its owner, Gouverneur Kemble, persuaded Parrott to leave the army and become the foundry's superintendent.

In 1839 Parrott married Kemble's sister, Mary, and leased the foundry from his brother-in-law. He bought 7,000 forested acres to assure his charcoal supply and acquired the Greenwood Iron Furnace for a steady source of pig iron.

Parrott also experimented with gun and shell designs. In 1861 he patented a rifled cannon, strengthened by a wrought-iron hoop around the rear of the barrel, and an expanding explosive shell. Offered at cost to the government, Parrott guns equipped Union land and naval forces throughout the Civil War.

If I were a younger man I should return to the army...[but as superintendent of the West Point Foundry] I can be of use and I intend that these guns shall cost the United States no more than is absolutely necessary.

ROBERT P. PARROTT, AFTER THE FIRST BATTLE OF BULL RUN, 21 JULY 1861

A Parrott rifle, used for siege work, mounted on a railway carriage

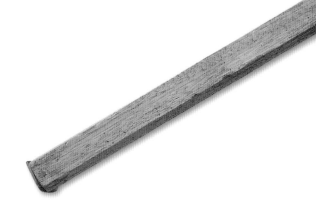

Model of a Parrott rifled cannon. Parrott guns in a variety of sizes were the most widely used rifled artillery of the Civil War.

Gunner's quadrant, an instrument for estimating range

Robert P. Parrott (Class of 1824) patented this shell for his muzzle-loading rifled cannon. When fired, its base expanded to fit the rifling. Without such a device, it would be too difficult to force a shell, which had to fit tightly for the rifling to work, down a rifled barrel from the muzzle.

ROBERT EDWARD LEE

1807–1870 • Class of 1829

Two years after West Point, Lee married the wealthy Mary Ann Randolph Custis, Martha Washington's granddaughter. She and the couple's seven children remained at Arlington, the Custis mansion, while Lee pursued a distinguished career.

Lee proved himself an able combat leader in the Mexican War, three times winning recognition for bravery and initiative. Acknowledged as one of the army's best officers, he was offered command of the Union army in 1861. After much soul-searching, he declined. Although personally opposed to secession, he followed his home state into rebellion.

Lee took command of the Army of Northern Virginia in 1862, winning remarkable victories against often superior Union forces until his defeat at Gettysburg. Lee's surrender at Appomattox in 1865 effectively ended the war, though other Confederate armies remained in the field.

❝*I have felt I ought not longer to retain my commission in the Army....Save in the defense of my native State, I never desire again to draw my sword.***❞**

ROBERT E. LEE TO WINFIELD SCOTT, 20 APRIL 1861

The McLean House, Virginia, where the surrender was signed, about 1865

In 1867 Louis Guillaume, a prominent French-born Richmond, Virginia, artist, painted
the surrender in the McLean House parlor at Appomattox Court House, Virginia.

JOSEPH REID ANDERSON

1813–1892   Class of 1836

A year after graduation, Anderson married Sally Archer, daughter of the post surgeon at Fort Monroe, Virginia. Seeking better prospects than army life promised, he resigned to work as a civil engineer with Virginia State Engineer Claude Crozet, onetime West Point professor of engineering (1817 to 1823).

In 1841 Anderson joined the Tredegar Iron Company in Richmond, eventually becoming its owner. By 1860 the foundry was one of the nation's largest, producing locomotives; boilers; cables; naval hardware; and cannon. When war came, it emerged as the industrial heart of the Confederacy.

Using slave and free labor, Anderson supervised ordnance and munitions production through most of the war. When Richmond fell in 1865, the Federal government confiscated the company, but Anderson regained control in 1867 and remained a prominent Virginia businessman.

We are a unit here [Tredegar Iron Works] in defense of our liberties and will die before subjugation.

JOSEPH REID ANDERSON, MAY 1861

WILLIAM TECUMSEH SHERMAN

1820–1891 · Class of 1840

After West Point, the Ohio-born Sherman served at southern posts as an artillery officer before the Mexican War brought him to California. Returning east in 1850, he married Ellen Ewing, daughter of the man who had raised him after his father's early death. They had eight children. Sherman resigned from the army in 1853, but struggled in civilian life until 1859, when he happily became head of the Louisiana Military Seminary.

Secession drove Sherman north and the outbreak of war brought him back to the army. He rose to prominence with Ulysses S. Grant in the Vicksburg and Chattanooga campaigns. When Grant moved east to take command of all Union armies, Sherman launched the drive through Georgia and the Carolinas that devastated the Confederacy and made him famous. After the war, he succeeded Grant as the army's commanding general.

ULYSSES SIMPSON GRANT

1822–1885   Class of 1843

As a cadet Grant excelled only in horsemanship, but he proved a brave and resourceful junior officer in the Mexican War. In 1848 he and Julia Dent married. They became inseparable and had four children. The oldest, Frederick, was also a West Point graduate (Class of 1871). Grant disliked peacetime army service and resigned in 1854, despite few prospects in civilian life.

With the Civil War Grant emerged as one of history's greatest generals. None of the war's other generals won the surrender of three enemy armies—at Fort Donelson (1862), Vicksburg (1863), and Appomattox (1865). No one else so effectively united strategic vision, operational finesse, tactical focus, exemplary leadership, moral courage, and unassuming modesty.

Twice elected president, Grant completed his masterly memoirs four days before his death from throat cancer.

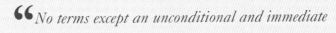

❝ *No terms except an unconditional and immediate surrender can be accepted.* **❞**

ULYSSES S. GRANT REPLYING TO WEST POINT CLASSMATE SIMON BOLIVAR BUCKNER'S REQUEST FOR SURRENDER TERMS AT FORT DONELSON, FEBRUARY 1862

Field glasses General Grant used during the Civil War

Gold membership badge in the Grand Army of the Republic awarded to U. S. Grant, 1879

Chairs used by Robert E. Lee (left) and Ulysses S. Grant (right) when they met at Appomattox Court House, Virginia, in 1865.

THOMAS JONATHAN "STONEWALL" JACKSON

1824–1863   Class of 1846

Jackson went directly from West Point into the Mexican War. The young artillerist twice won commendation for courage in battle, rising to the temporary rank of major. Unhappy in the peacetime army, he resigned in 1851 to become a professor at the Virginia Military Institute.

Austere and devout, Jackson disdained gambling, drinking, and smoking. He married twice, both times a Presbyterian minister's daughter. Elinor Junkin, his first wife, married him in 1853 but died little more than a year later. He wed Mary Anne Morrison in 1857, and the couple had a daughter, Julia.

Jackson's short Civil War career began with the brilliant Shenandoah Valley campaign in 1862, and he achieved almost mythic proportions as Robert E. Lee's great partner. It ended with an accidental shooting by his own troops at the Battle of Chancellorsville in May 1863.

I trust God will grant us a great victory. Keep closed on Chancellorsville.

STONEWALL JACKSON, FINAL ORDERS TO J.E.B. STUART, 1 MAY 1863

THE ARMY IN RECONSTRUCTION

FEDERAL troops were stationed throughout the defeated Confederacy to maintain order and ensure compliance with Federal law. It was no easy task for small army detachments in isolated regions, such as Capt. Thomas Tolman's (Class of 1865) unit in Sulphur Springs, Texas.

A central issue was the place of freed slaves in the reconstructed South. Congress created the Freedmen's Bureau in 1865 to prepare newly liberated slaves for responsible citizenship. The reality was different. Headed by O. O. Howard (Class of 1854) and backed by military force, the bureau's chief function became protecting freedmen against racist violence.

African American soldiers had become a significant part of Union armies during the war, 12 percent of total manpower by 1865. They continued to serve as part of the postwar regular army, and in 1870 Congress directed West Point to admit African American cadets.

❝*I finally told them they must take their choice of enforcing their own laws or having them enforced by the military.***❞**

W. P. PEASE, CAPT. 17TH INFANTRY, COMMANDING POST OF SULPHUR SPRINGS, TEXAS, REPORT TO COMMANDING GENERAL, 5TH MILITARY DISTRICT, AUSTIN, TEXAS, 3 OCTOBER 1868

This 1872 photograph shows the surviving stockade fence and officers' quarters of the 1868 Federal stockade in Sulphur Springs, Texas.

OLIVER OTIS HOWARD

1830–1909 • Class of 1854

Howard completed four years at Bowdoin College before attending West Point. Unlike many northern graduates, he stayed in the army. Two years later he married Elizabeth Ann Waite (below); they had two children. Howard soon returned to West Point to teach mathematics, a tour of duty cut short by war.

Well connected politically, he rose rapidly to corps command, despite losing his right arm in an 1862 battle. Strong religious, civil rights, and temperance views led to his choice as head of the new Freedmen's Bureau in 1865. His record as commissioner was, like his army record, mixed. But a real concern for African American education made him active in founding Howard University. Spending the 1870s in several western Indian campaigns, Howard became West Point superintendent in 1881.

THOMAS MURRAY TOLMAN

1841–1883   Class of 1865

Thomas Murray Tolman (center) with members of his unit, "Tolman's Thirty"

Appointed to West Point from Maine, Tolman arrived just after the Civil War began and graduated just after it ended. Assigned to frontier duty with the 6th Cavalry in Texas, he rose to the rank of captain before reaching Sulphur Springs in April 1869.

Bands of proslavery outlaws within the small town and surrounding Hopkins County fiercely contested Federal authority during Reconstruction. Federal troops were unwelcome, and violence escalated. Tolman responded by forming a special thirty-man unit, "Tolman's Thirty," to enforce Federal law and suppress disorder.

Their stern measures provoked complaints and may have skirted the law. Before the end of the year, Tolman was suspended from command, charged with mistreating a prisoner. After a year's confinement within Fort Jefferson, he returned to active duty and left Texas.

The victory parade of Union troops down
Pennsylvania Avenue in Washington, D.C.

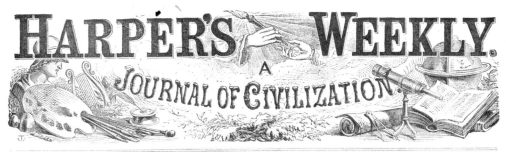

HARPER'S WEEKLY.
A JOURNAL OF CIVILIZATION.

Vol. XI.—No. 568.]   NEW YORK, SATURDAY, NOVEMBER 16, 1867.   [SINGLE COPIES TEN CENTS.
[$4.00 PER YEAR IN ADVANCE.

Entered according to Act of Congress, in the Year 1867, by Harper & Brothers, in the Clerk's Office of the District Court for the Southern District of New York.

"THE FIRST VOTE."—Drawn by A. R. Waud.—[See next Page.]

Former slaves obtained the right to vote, if they were male.

4

AN ARMY
FOR THE NATION

BETWEEN THE CIVIL WAR and World War I, West Point graduates were the heart of the army's officer corps. They became increasingly professionalized and effective, as they proved in the Spanish-American War. From the late 1860s until the 1890s, the United States maintained only a small army of 25,000, its officers mostly West Pointers. With little prospect of foreign war, the army's duties were chiefly limited to completing the conquest of the Native Americans, maintaining order in labor disputes and other so-called domestic disorders, and performing ceremonial functions.

The U.S. Army became increasingly career-oriented, technically proficient, and nonpolitical during the late 19th century. West Pointers strongly promoted schools for the advanced training of officers in their areas of specialization, which the army began to establish in the 1880s. The Spanish-American War and the Philippine War that followed resulted in a larger regular army and further reforms. West Pointers were in the forefront of efforts to establish the War Department General Staff and Army War College. They also contributed to the organization of the National Guard.

During the 1902 centennial celebrations at West Point, President Theodore Roosevelt pinned the Medal of Honor onto Calvin P. Titus, an army trumpeter, for his heroism during the Boxer Rebellion in China in 1900.

THE ARMY IN THE WEST

AFTER the Civil War, much of the army went to the West, stationed far from public view. The army's chief task was mediating between the swelling flood of white settlers and the Native Americans whose livelihoods, ways of life, and lives themselves were threatened.

West Point provided most of the officers, with the rank and file recruited heavily from immigrants and African Americans. Hierarchy reigned in the frontier army. Officers did not mingle socially with their men, nor did their wives and children have much to do with enlisted families.

Garrisons were usually small, rarely more than a few companies, and they were widely scattered. Isolated, poorly paid, often inadequately housed, and very slow to win promotion, bachelor and married officers alike found life on frontier posts harsh, as did military wives and children. Duty was mostly routine, and disability or death was far more likely from disease than combat.

> **Though I had not desired the colored infantry . . . I have never regretted my service in that regiment.**
>
> CHARLES J. CRANE (CLASS OF 1877),
> ON HIS ASSIGNMENT TO THE 24TH
> INFANTRY

The parade ground at Fort D. A. Russell, near Cheyenne, Wyoming

GEORGE CROOK

1829–1890   Class of 1852

After graduating from West Point, Crook continued his army career on the West Coast, where he came to respect the Indians he was sent to subdue. "When they were pushed beyond endurance and would go on the warpath, we had to fight when our sympathies were with the Indians," he later wrote. As a senior officer he became an outspoken champion of Indian rights.

Crook distinguished himself in the Civil War, rising to the rank of major general, but returned to the frontier when the war ended. Among his notable innovations was substituting pack mules for wagon trains to supply his troops. As the photograph suggests (inset below), he also preferred riding mules to horses.

More controversially, Crook used Indian scouts and auxiliaries extensively. He also preferred negotiation to armed force in dealing with the problems arising from white settlement and the often unfair treatment that Indians received.

GEORGE ARMSTRONG CUSTER

1839–1876 ✦ Class of 1861

Although Custer graduated at the bottom of his class of June 1861, he immediately distinguished himself in the Civil War as a flamboyant, heedlessly brave cavalry officer. At age twenty-three he held the temporary rank of major general, the youngest in the Union army. In 1864 he married Elizabeth ("Libbie") Bacon, a Michigan judge's daughter, bright and well educated.

After the war, Libbie accompanied her husband to his assignment as commander of the 7th Cavalry. For the next decade, the Custers led exciting lives, establishing homes at several frontier army posts.

Ever the aggressive soldier, Custer blundered into more than he could handle at the Battle of the Little Bighorn (25 June 1876), where he and much of the 7th Cavalry met their deaths. As his widow, Libbie Custer devoted herself tirelessly in print and lecture to embellishing the legend of her husband as a great military hero.

George and Libbie Custer and their maid Eliza (left)

Libbie Custer gave this buckskin coat worn by her husband to the Smithsonian.

Custer's wicker hamper

Shortly before the Battle of the Little Bighorn, Custer's officers and their wives sat for a photographer.

Custer's Last Fight, an 1896 lithograph by F. Otto Becker widely distributed by the Anheuser-Busch Brewing Company, has become one of the best-known depictions of the legendary battle.

RANALD SLIDELL MACKENZIE

1840–1889 • Class of 1862

Mackenzie went directly from classroom to battlefield. By the end of the Civil War, he had been wounded six times, cited for gallantry seven times, and risen to major general of volunteers. Grant thought him the army's "most promising young officer."

After the war Mackenzie became colonel of the newly formed 41st (later the 24th) Infantry, one of the regular army's first black units. Judged by many to be a dubious experiment, the regiment under Mackenzie's discipline and training proved itself along the Mexican border.

In 1871 Mackenzie assumed command of the 4th Cavalry, his main task forcing Indians back to their reservations. Operating in Texas, Mexico, Wyoming, Colorado, Utah, and New Mexico, his highly successful strategy focused less on shedding blood than on destroying horses and other property. Mental illness forced Mackenzie into retirement in 1884.

> *He was always prompt in the saddle and never tangled his spurs in the maze of red tape.*

EULOGY FOR RANALD MACKENZIE BY A TEXAS JOURNALIST, 1889

FAYETTE WASHINGTON ROE

1850–1916 ★ Class of 1871

Roe's family came from upstate New York, though he was born in Virginia. When he graduated from West Point, he married another upstate New Yorker, Frances Mack. Roe's first assignment took the couple west to Colorado, and over the next fifteen years to Montana, Utah, and the Dakotas.

Roe's military career was an unremarkable series of clerical and administrative posts. He would have passed into obscurity had he not appeared as Frances's beloved comrade "Faye" in her lively and perceptive account of frontier life, *Army Letters from an Officer's Wife* (1909).

Captivated by the beauty of western landscapes, Frances described in telling detail the scenes and events in their army communities. She carefully balanced tales of lively social life with attention to the harsh conditions and isolation that military families endured.

❝*We will see that the tents are made comfortable and cheerful at every camp, that the little dinner after the weary march, the early breakfast and the cold luncheon one and all are as dainty as camp cooking will permit.***❞**

FRANCES ROE, *ARMY LETTERS FROM AN OFFICER'S WIFE*, 1909

Frances Roe wears her husband's cadet jacket, which she remodeled to fit herself.

An army laundress and her sergeant husband

Black troops normally had white officers in the 19th century.

Young Indian woman
carrying sticks

HENRY OSSIAN FLIPPER

1856–1940 ★ Class of 1877

West Point opened to African American men in 1870, another of Reconstruction's short-lived gains. Flipper was the first of only three black graduates before 1900. Hostility from fellow cadets and formidable academic demands made his graduation and commissioning an extraordinary achievement, described in his book, *The Colored Cadet at West Point* (1878).

Although Flipper became the regular army's first black officer, his brief career was controversial. He was dismissed in 1882 for "conduct unbecoming an officer and a gentleman," but a presidential pardon in 1999 absolved him of the questionable charges that cost him an army career.

Flipper prospered in civilian life, surveying and speculating in Texas and Mexican land. In 1891 he and Luisa Montoya entered into an Arizona marriage contract. Territorial law prohibited interracial marriage but allowed contract relationships.

WARS FOR EMPIRE

CUBANS seeking independence from Spain launched guerrilla war in 1895. The Spanish crackdown alienated American public opinion, making war all but inevitable after the battleship *Maine* exploded and sank in Havana harbor. The United States declared war on 25 April 1898, and West Point hurriedly graduated that year's class the next day.

A huge influx of volunteers, including such former Confederates as Fitzhugh Lee (Class of 1856) and Joseph Wheeler (Class of 1859), multiplied an army of 26,000 by more than ten. West Point graduates served at every level from lieutenant to general, not only in fighting but in postwar administration of Cuba and Puerto Rico.

The war also removed Spain from the Philippines, but Filipinos fighting for independence since 1896 saw Americans only as new masters. Although war with Spain ended in 1899, the Philippine War lasted until 1902 and sporadic violence continued for years. Again West Pointers played large roles, both as fighters and administrators.

"*It has been a splendid little war.*"

SECRETARY OF STATE JOHN HAY TO COL. THEODORE ROOSEVELT, 27 JULY 1898 (THE DAY AFTER THE FALL OF SANTIAGO)

Frontline troops in Cuba relied on pack trains of mules for supplies.

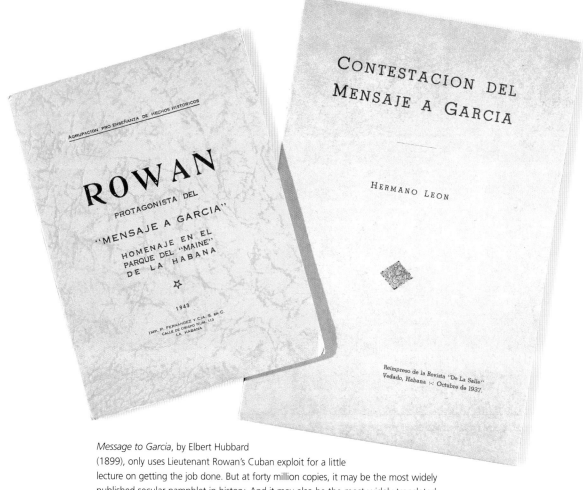

AGRUPACION PRO ENSEÑANZA DE HECHOS HISTORICOS

ROWAN

PROTAGONISTA DEL
"MENSAJE A GARCIA"

HOMENAJE EN EL
PARQUE DEL "MAINE"
DE LA HABANA

☆

1943

IMP. P. FERNANDEZ Y CIA. S. EN C.
CALLE DE OBISPO NUM. 113
LA HABANA

CONTESTACION DEL
MENSAJE A GARCIA

HERMANO LEON

Reimpreso de la Revista "De La Salle"
Vedado, Habana :-: Octubre de 1937.

Message to Garcia, by Elbert Hubbard
(1899), only uses Lieutenant Rowan's Cuban exploit for a little
lecture on getting the job done. But at forty million copies, it may be the most widely
published secular pamphlet in history. And it may also be the most widely translated,
with versions in some 70 languages. It has also inspired two feature movies.

Most regular troops carried the Krag-Jorgensen, a Danish
model adopted by the U.S. Army as its first magazine rifle.

Filipinos fighting the U.S. Army sometimes
resorted to making their own firearms.

ANDREW SUMMERS ROWAN

1857–1943 Class of 1881

Rowan's army career was, for the most part, unremarkable: garrison duty at various posts in the United States; some survey work in Central America; a Washington assignment in the Adjutant General's Office; appointment as military attaché to Chile; staff service in Puerto Rico and Cuba during the War with Spain; some time in the Philippines; a year teaching military science in Kansas; and retirement as major after thirty years service.

There was one spectacular break in the routine. Early in 1898, Rowan was dispatched on a secret mission to obtain information on the strength of rebel forces in Cuba from their leader, Gen. Calixto Garcia. Rowan landed on the island the day Spain declared war, found Garcia, and returned with the information in eleven days. Rowan's exploit inspired a much-reprinted and much-translated 1899 pamphlet by Elbert Hubbard, *Message to Garcia*, which made the officer's name world famous.

FRANK ROSS McCOY

1874–1954 ★ Class of 1897

Assigned to the 10th Cavalry (African American) after graduating from West Point, McCoy saw action in Cuba and was wounded at San Juan Hill. In the Philippines, he led a daring 1905 raid into the jungle that killed the rebel Moro chieftain Datu Ali and many of his followers. He later saw combat along the Mexican border and commanded a brigade in World War I.

But McCoy's most notable achievements were political and diplomatic. A protégé of Gen. Leonard Wood and President Theodore Roosevelt, McCoy's civil-military duties spanned three decades: directing relief efforts after the 1923 Tokyo earthquake; supervising elections and maintaining public order in Nicaragua in 1927; delegate to the 1928 Pan-American Conference; working for the League of Nations; heading the Foreign Policy Association; and negotiating terms of the American occupation of Japan after World War II .

> ❝ *[Datu Ali] was a soldier and a gentleman....I don't blame him for fighting for his 'ancient customs.'* ❞

FRANK R. MCCOY TO HIS FAMILY, 3 DECEMBER 1903

These doctors and nurses with their patients, along with other medical personnel, played vital roles in the Spanish-American War. Disease killed far more soldiers than enemy fire.

Gatling Guns in Action, by Charles Johnson Post

Special Detail under Captain Rafferty Going into Santiago, by Charles Johnson Post. Appointed to West Point from Illinois, William Carroll Rafferty was commissioned in the artillery at graduation in 1880. He received his promotion to captain in March 1899, just a few months before Post captured his image. Rafferty retired from the army twenty years later as a colonel, just after the end of World War I.

In 1908 the "Wright Flyer", shown here over Fort Myer, Virginia, with Orville
Wright at the controls, became the army's first airplane purchase. Wright himself
trained the first army pilot, Frank Lahm (Class of 1901).

The tommy gun had only limited military roles, but achieved notoriety as "the gun that made the twenties roar." Formally the Thompson submachine gun, it was named after its inventor, John Taliaferro Thompson (Class of 1882).

War Department certificate for Frank Lahm, the first army pilot.

MONUMENTAL PROJECTS

I N the decades between Reconstruction and World War I, West Pointers engaged in a number of large-scale building projects. Once again, their engineering education served national and local needs as they rebuilt the Philadelphia waterworks and supervised the New York park system.

Graduates of West Point also played significant roles in reshaping the city of Washington, D.C., with such major additions to the urban landscape as the Washington Monument, the Library of Congress, and Rock Creek Parkway.

Perhaps most epic of all, they linked the Atlantic and Pacific Oceans with a canal through the Isthmus of Panama. The Panama Canal was a huge engineering enterprise. West Pointers assumed key positions after George Goethals (Class of 1880) became chief engineer of the project in 1907. He assembled a senior staff of other West Pointers and sprinkled more junior officers throughout the project.

"*Everything is on a colossal scale.***"**

SCIENTIFIC AMERICAN, 18 MARCH 1911

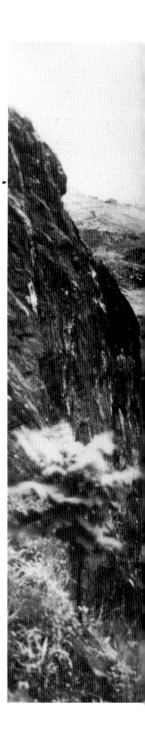

This photograph shows the Culebra Cut, a section of the Panama Canal, as a work in progress in June 1913, a year before the canal opened. The Culebra Cut was excavated through the backbone of the Isthmus of Panama, nine miles of solid rock covered with waterlogged and unstable earth prone to massive slides. David Gaillard (Class of 1884) did the job with an army of some 6,000 diggers, fifty to sixty steam shovels, and an endless stream of railroad cars to haul the dirt away.

THOMAS LINCOLN CASEY

1831–1896 ★ Class of 1852

The son of Gen. Silas Casey (Class of 1826), Thomas and his two brothers became career officers, while his two sisters married army officers. After graduating from West Point, he spent his career in the Corps of Engineers. In 1856, while teaching engineering at West Point, he married Emma Weir, daughter of eminent artist Robert W. Weir, who taught at West Point. The Caseys had three sons, the oldest following his grandfather and father to West Point (Class of 1879).

After building seacoast fortifications during the Civil War, Casey came to Washington D.C., in 1867 to head the Division of Fortifications. In 1877 he took over the District of Columbia's Office of Public Buildings and Grounds. During the next two decades, he oversaw such major building projects as the Washington Monument; the State, War, and Navy Building (now the Eisenhower Executive Office Building); and the Library of Congress.

Shortly before Lt. Col. Thomas L. Casey took over the Office of Public Buildings and Grounds for the District of Columbia in 1877, Congress decided that the Washington Monument should be completed. The monument's bankrupt sponsors had abandoned the project in 1855, leaving behind a poorly designed 173-foot stub on a faulty foundation. Casey set to work in 1878, correcting the foundation, redesigning the monument, and then supervising the construction. (The photograph captures the work in progress.) In December 1884 Casey marked the project's completion by personally capping the 555-foot monument with a 100-ounce block of what was then a very rare and expensive metal only recently discovered—aluminum.

GEORGE WASHINGTON GOETHALS

1858–1928 • Class of 1880

After graduating from West Point, Goethals enjoyed a solid career as an army engineer, including two tours of duty teaching engineering at West Point. In 1903 he joined the newly created War Department General Staff.

In 1907, he was appointed chief engineer of the Panama Canal project. Placing West Pointers in key positions, he brought it in ahead of schedule. It opened for traffic in 1914. Goethals, now famous, remained in the Canal Zone as governor until he retired in 1916.

Recalled to active duty in World War I, Goethals became acting quartermaster general and director of the general staff's purchase, storage, and traffic division. From this relatively obscure post, he brought the army's vast supply system under central control.

Again retired after the Armistice, Goethals became a successful engineering consultant in New York.

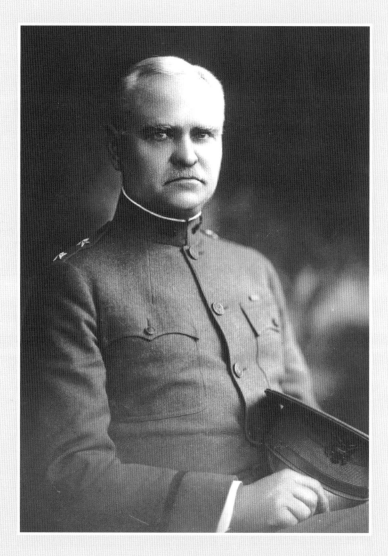

> **❝** *I now consider that I am commanding the Army of Panama, and that the enemy we are both going to combat is the Culebra Cut and the locks and dams at both ends of the canal.* **❞**

GEORGE W. GOETHALS, QUOTED IN *PANAMA STAR & HERALD*, 19 MARCH 1907

DAVID DUBOSE GAILLARD

1859–1913 • Class of 1884

Until 1903 Gaillard enjoyed a solid and typical army engineering career. After graduation from West Point and promotion to first lieutenant in 1887, he married Katherine Ross Davis; the couple had one child. In 1903 Gaillard was appointed to the new General Staff Corps, where he met his future boss, George Goethals. When Goethals went to Panama in 1907, he brought Gaillard along.

Goethals's reorganization of canal construction placed Gaillard in charge of the notorious Culebra Cut through the backbone of the isthmus. He succeeded, but did not live to see the job finished. Suffering from what was thought to be nervous exhaustion brought on by overwork, he returned to the United States in 1913. In fact, Gaillard had suffered a fatal brain tumor. The Panama Canal opened nine months after his death, and Culebra Cut was renamed Gaillard Cut in his honor.

5

AMERICA IN THE GREAT WAR

DURING WORLD WAR I, West Point graduates held almost all top command and staff posts. They were in charge of raising the troops, supplying them, and leading them in combat. Although the United States became an imperial power after the Spanish-American War, its armed forces stayed small by European standards. The nation remained neutral during World War I until 1917, when perceived German provocation, especially the U-boat war, induced the United States to join the Allies. Only then did large-scale mobilization begin, including, for the first time, women.

Unlike previous American wars, World War I saw no political generals. Professionals were fully in charge. West Pointers held almost all the top command and staff posts, both at home and abroad. They managed the entire American war effort, from mobilizing the nation's human and economic resources to assembling the fighting forces and leading them in combat. By spring 1918, hundreds of thousands of citizen soldiers were in Europe. Fresh American troops proved decisive in ending the war. A mature America now had proved itself a Great Power.

On the Job for Victory poster by artist Jonas Lie reflects the idea of military victory based on industrial production (detail).

SUPPLYING THE ARMY

"AMATEURS study tactics," goes an old saying, "armchair generals study strategy, but professionals study logistics [obtaining and moving supplies]." A wave of reform, stimulated by the logistic failures of the Spanish-American War and sustained by the Progressive Movement, swept the army in the decade before World War I. The more tightly run, businesslike army administration that emerged included reorganized supply services, although significant elements of the old independent bureau system remained intact.

On the eve of America's entry into the war, three major bureaus provided the army with its supplies and equipment. The Quartermaster Corps under Henry Sharpe (Class of 1880) provided and distributed food, clothing, and everything else the army needed except munitions and communications. All aspects of weapons and ammunition, from design to maintenance, belonged to the Ordnance Corps under William Crozier (Class of 1876). The Signal Corps under George Squier (Class of 1887) was responsible for communications gear and airplanes.

"At first there will be increased slaughter—increased slaughter on so terrible a scale as to render it impossible to push the battle to a decisive issue. . . . Then, instead of a war fought out to the bitter end in a series of decisive battles, we shall have to substitute a long period of continually increasing strain upon the resources of the combatants. . . . That is the future of war—not fighting but famine, not the slaying of men but the bankruptcy of nations and the break-up of the whole social organization."

JEAN DE BLOCH, *IS WAR NOW IMPOSSIBLE? THE FUTURE OF WAR IN ITS TECHNICAL, ECONOMIC AND POLITICAL RELATIONS,* 1899

Members of the 325th Field Signal Battalion string wire in no-man's-land.

WILLIAM CROZIER

1855–1942 · Class of 1876

Crozier's career began with three years in the West and eight years teaching mathematics at West Point. Reassigned to the office of the chief of ordnance in 1887, he helped improve coastal artillery with such inventions as the disappearing gun carriage. After field service in the Philippines and China, he returned to West Point.

In 1901 President Theodore Roosevelt plucked Captain Crozier from West Point to become a brigadier general and chief of ordnance, a position he held until 1918. Crozier made Federal armories testing grounds for new weapons and more efficient manufacturing techniques.

Recognizing the growing interdependence of ordnance and civil science, engineering, and industry, he became a forceful advocate of industrial preparedness. His efforts paid off handsomely in World War I. Crozier played a vital role organizing the conversion of civilian factories for ordnance production.

❝*[Before the war, army officers] had no experience in searching out manufacturing facilities, in bargaining for just prices, or in allocating to one another, in accordance with their respective needs, a limited capacity for production.***❞**

MAJ. GEN. WILLIAM CROZIER, *ORDNANCE AND THE WORLD WAR,* 1920

HENRY GRANVILLE SHARPE

1858–1947   Class of 1880

Sharpe moved to the Commissary Corps three years after graduation and for the next fifteen years handled food supply at a number of army posts. In the Spanish-American War, his good work at Camp Thomas, Georgia, then in Puerto Rico, and finally in the Philippines, contrasted sharply with the army's generally dismal logistical performance.

Named commissary general in 1905, Sharpe sought to improve army rations and food preparation. In 1912 the new Quartermaster Corps absorbed his department, a reform he favored. Four years later Sharpe became quartermaster general.

When the United States declared war, Sharpe faced the formidable challenge of housing, feeding, clothing, and equipping a massively expanded army. He made great progress, but not fast enough to meet political demands. In December 1917 he was replaced by George Goethals (Class of 1880).

" *I wish I could have had a clearer and more helpful view of some of the tremendous difficulties with which you were beset.* **"**

FORMER SECRETARY OF WAR NEWTON D. BAKER TO HENRY G. SHARPE, 29 AUGUST 1921

GEORGE OWEN SQUIER

1865–1934 • Class of 1887

Squier followed graduation from West Point with advanced study at Baltimore's Johns Hopkins University, becoming in 1893 the army's first Ph.D. Forty years of electrical research, including several basic radio patents, won him membership in the National Academy of Sciences.

Squier in 1905 established the army's first signals school at Fort Leavenworth, Kansas, and later the army's radio research laboratory at Fort Monmouth, New Jersey. He also pioneered army aviation, writing the first specifications for a military airplane in 1907 and later founding the army's aviation research laboratory at Langley Field, Virginia.

Appointed chief signal officer in 1917, Squier oversaw all army communications and aviation in World War I. Although his reputation took a bruising from wartime problems with aircraft production over which he had little control, Squier deserves great credit for institutionalizing research in the army.

> **"**Now that Mr. Wright is accomplishing such wonders in the air almost anything in the aeronautical line seems possible.**"**

GEORGE O. SQUIER IN *WASHINGTON POST* INTERVIEW, SEPTEMBER 1908

Assembling Liberty Planes at Romarantin, pencil sketch by J. A. Smith

Rail-head Dump at Menil-la-Tour, pastel sketch by J. A. Smith

Samples of quartermaster-supplied items include belt webbing, a canteen, and a gas mask

Munitions manufacturing was the key war industry. With strong encouragement from Chief of Ordnance William Crozier, American industry became a major ally supplier of munitions like the 75-mm shell shown here.

MOBILIZING MANPOWER AND INDUSTRY

MILITARY mobilization means assembling and organizing troops, supplies, and equipment for war. In World War I, the scope of mobilization expanded beyond all previous experience. Producing and distributing the vast amounts of supplies, equipment, and munitions required by armies of millions became a central goal of war-making across Europe.

New terms like "total war" and "home front" testified to the new importance of industrial capacity and to the extension of military control over much of civic life. As more officers became rear-echelon managers rather than front-line leaders, they increasingly saw their goal as outlasting rather than outmaneuvering the enemy.

These European developments prodded West Pointers into thinking about mobilization and how to accomplish it in the United States. From 1914 to 1917 planning centered in the War Department under chiefs of staff Hugh L. Scott (Class of 1876) and Tasker H. Bliss (Class of 1875).

> *"Before the end it was found necessary to establish a very comprehensive scheme of control over the entire industrial life of the Nation, and indeed toward the end control was extending beyond our borders to every part of the world from which war supplies were drawn."*
>
> BERNARD M. BARUCH, *AMERICAN INDUSTRY IN THE WAR: A REPORT OF THE WAR INDUSTRIES BOARD*, MARCH 1921

De Haviland fighter planes with Liberty engines were manufactured at the Dayton-Wright Company in Ohio.

HUGH LENOX SCOTT

1853–1934 ★ Class of 1876

After graduating from West Point, Scott spent the next two decades of his military career in the frontier cavalry, capped by five years recruiting and commanding an Apache, Kiowa, and Comanche cavalry troop. He later wrote a definitive treatise on the sign language of the Plains Indians under the auspices of the Smithsonian Institution's Bureau of American Ethnology.

The Spanish-American War shifted Scott's career in new directions. From 1898 to 1906, he served first as adjutant general in Cuba, then as a military governor in the Philippines. He returned to a four-year term as superintendent of West Point.

After commanding cavalry along the Mexican border, Scott came to Washington in 1914 as army chief of staff. He directed war preparations and helped develop the Selective Service System of conscription.

ENOCH HERBERT CROWDER

1859–1932   Class of 1881

No sooner had Crowder joined the frontier cavalry than he began studying for the law degree that redirected his career. Transferred to the Judge Advocate Corps, he oversaw a thorough updating of the Articles of War and the Manual for Courts Martial. Eventually Crowder became judge advocate general.

When war in Europe after 1914 showed that America's reliance on volunteers would not produce the huge numbers that modern war seemed to demand, Crowder helped draft and implement the 1917 Selective Service Act. Reasonably equitable and administered chiefly by civilian volunteers in local draft boards, it was conscription with a human face that avoided the Civil War's widespread opposition and violence. The draft registered almost 24 million men and called about 2.8 million into service—four-fifths of the army raised by the United States in World War I .

"*Every man in the draft age must work or fight.***"**

ENOCH H. CROWDER, INSTRUCTIONS TO DRAFT BOARDS, 1917

WE ARE THE RESERVE ARMY U.S. 16 MEN

To dramatize the country's military weakness in 1915, Massachusetts Congressman A. P. Gardner invited the army's entire enlisted reserve—sixteen men—to dinner at a Washington Hotel.

Many thousands of civilian women volunteered for wartime service and donned military-style uniforms, such as this one from the American Library Association.

First World War industrial mobilization opened new opportunities for these welders and other women workers.

HUGH SAMUEL JOHNSON

1882–1942   Class of 1903

Aside from writing popular stories about military and western life, Johnson had a seemingly routine career in the frontier cavalry until 1914. Then Judge Advocate General Enoch Crowder (Class of 1881) sent him to law school. Johnson assisted Crowder in planning and implementing the Selective Service System.

In 1918 Johnson moved to the War Department General Staff, working under Quartermaster General George Goethals (Class of 1880) to reorganize army procurement. Representing Goethals on the War Industries Board, he contributed significantly to America's first successful integration of military and industrial sectors behind a massive wartime buildup. In his wartime work, Johnson proved himself an able second-in-command.

Johnson resigned in 1919 to pursue a business career, but returned to public service in 1933 under the New Deal to head the National Recovery Administration.

66 *The nearest thing to immortality in this world is a government bureau. A bureaucrat's idea of cleaning up his files is to make a copy of every paper before he destroys it.* 99

HUGH S. JOHNSON, 1933

AMERICA AT WAR

WORLD War I displayed the consequences of industrial growth and expanding mechanization. Vast armies supplied by railroad and motor vehicle from seemingly endless production lines faced stalemate. Magazine rifles and machine guns backed by quick-firing artillery drove armies to ground. Trench warfare, more siege than battle, marked the triumph of the engineers and artillerists. It was a kind of war for which West Point training seemed especially apt.

The American Expeditionary Force would break this deadlock imposed by mechanized firepower—as soon as General John Pershing (Class of 1886) built an independent American army. Although he refused to feed American replacements into depleted Allied units, the swelling numbers of American troops still boosted Allied morale and demoralized the enemy. Large-scale American combat began only in summer 1918. It speeded the final exhaustion of German reserves and the Armistice on 11 November that ended the war, much sooner than expected.

"In order that the estimates and plans regarding our participation should be realized, this organization behind the lines would have to become a great army in itself. . . . The success of a military commander depends largely upon . . . managing the business of transportation and supply."

JOHN J. PERSHING, *MY EXPERIENCES IN THE WORLD WAR*, 1931

American troops in Alsace, 29 August 1918, are equipped with a French-made Choucrot machine gun.

JOHN JOSEPH PERSHING

1860–1948   Class of 1886

When Captain Pershing married Frances Warren in 1905, he had served in the frontier cavalry, taught at West Point, ridden with the 10th (Colored) Cavalry in Cuba, and distinguished himself in the Philippines. In 1906 he became brigadier general, an unusual peacetime promotion bestowed by his friend, President Theodore Roosevelt, and his father-in-law, Francis E. Warren, chairman of the Senate Military Affairs Committee.

In August 1915, with Pershing in El Paso, Texas, organizing a hunt for bandits in Mexico, Frances and their three daughters perished in a fire. His son survived, but the tragedy made a hard man even less compromising.

As American commander in France, Pershing repulsed all attempts to replace Allied losses with American troops. Vindicated by victory only months after full-scale American assaults began, Pershing became only the fourth five-star general and a world-renowned figure.

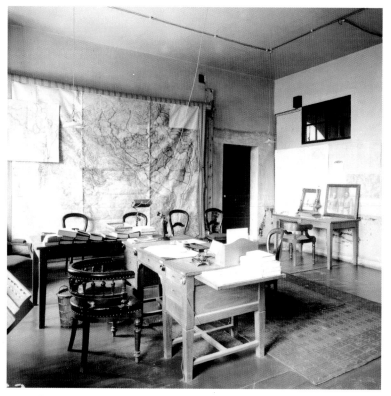

J. J. Pershing's war room at Chaumont, France

Unloading stores of "canned willie [sausage]" and hardtack

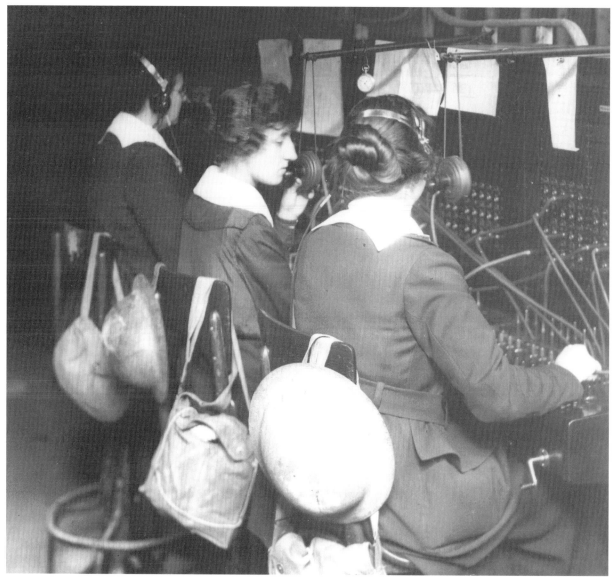

Bilingual telephone operators, called "hello girls," operate
the switchboard in Chaumont, headquarters of the American
Expeditionary Force in France. Although employed by the U.S.
Army Signal Corps, they did not receive the regular army pay
and benefits they expected.

> **"***Instead of trying to train men of the Signal Corps, I requested that a number of experienced telephone girls who could speak French be sent over. . . . Some doubt existed among the members of the staff as to the wisdom of this step, but it soon vanished as the increased efficiency of our telephone system became apparent.***"**
>
> JOHN J. PERSHING, *MY EXPERIENCES IN THE WORLD WAR*, 1931

This is the Signal Corps uniform worn by the bilingual female telephone operators, the so-called "hello girls" requested by General Pershing for service in France.

Despite the development of motorized transport, mules still
formed the backbone of the frontline supply system

Armband authorized for members of the general staff section
in Pershing's headquarters

PEYTON CONWAY MARCH

1864–1955   Class of 1888

Commissioned in artillery after graduation from West Point, March proved an able combat commander in the Spanish-American and Philippine Wars, repeatedly cited for gallantry and recommended for the medal of honor.

In 1903 he was selected for the new War Department General Staff. When America entered World War I, March became chief of artillery in the American Expeditionary Force.

Recalled to Washington as the army's chief of staff in March 1918, March held an expansive view of his authority. That brought endless clashes with General Pershing commanding the field army, but also greatly advanced the war effort. March reorganized the general staff, bolstered logistics, established new technical branches to reflect the new kind of war—Air Service, Tank Corps, Motor Transport Corps, and Chemical Warfare Service—and, above all, orchestrated manpower mobilization to create the mass army that industrial warfare required.

❝ *We are going to win the war if it takes every man in the United States.* **❞**

PEYTON C. MARCH, QUOTED IN THE *NEW YORK TIMES*, 16 AUGUST 1918

CHARLES PELOT SUMMERALL

1867–1955 ★ Class of 1892

Summerall transferred from infantry to artillery a few months after graduation. He saw combat in the Philippines and China. Returning to West Point in 1905, he taught artillery tactics for six years. He then commanded summer camps of instruction for army and National Guard artillery before assignment to the general staff in 1914.

America's entry into World War I brought Summerall command of a field artillery brigade that first saw action in France at Cantigny. In 1918 he assumed command of the 1st Division in the Soissons and St. Mihiel operations, then of V Corps in the Meuse-Argonne offensive.

Summerall retired in 1931 as army chief of staff. For the next 22 years, he served as president of The Citadel, a military college n Charleston, South Carolina.

66 *There has been...a tendency to exaggerate losses and casualties by the use of [such] expressions [as]: 'All shot to pieces.' All officers and soldiers are forbidden to use such expressions in official messages, reports, conversations or discussions.* 99

MAJ. GEN. CHARLES P. SUMMERALL, *V CORPS DIRECTIVE*, 1918

American infantry advancing with tanks

American troops relied on Allied sources for this French Choucrot machine gun and much of their other equipment.

6

WEST POINT IN THE 20TH CENTURY

WEST POINT CHANGED to meet the demands of a new century. World War I mobilization seriously disrupted the Academy. Appointed superintendent after the Armistice, Douglas MacArthur (Class of 1903) oversaw the Academy's restoration to good health. Although World War II proved less damaging to normal functioning, it stimulated even more far-reaching reforms, first by Maxwell Taylor (Class of 1922), then by Garrison Davidson (Class of 1927).

West Point's 20th-century curriculum grew to include a new range of subjects required of the well-schooled officer. Until the 1950s, everyone took the same courses. Now cadets may choose among many. Who might become an officer also changed. After mid-century West Point's doors opened wider, first to African Americans and other minority men, then in 1976 to the formerly excluded women of America. By the end of the 20th century, West Point's faculty and corps of cadets had become far more representative of the nation they served than had been true in the 19th century.

West Point graduates
throwing their hats
into the air (detail)

RESTORING THE ACADEMY

IN the massive mobilization of World War I, the United States Military Academy was almost destroyed. As class after class graduated early and graduating classes were added, West Point more resembled an officers' training school than a military academy, its larger educational mission almost lost.

The postwar reestablishment under a new superintendent, Douglas MacArthur (Class of 1903), began a new era in the institution's history. MacArthur's reforms reinvigorated the Academy and helped prepare it for a new role.

For over a century, West Point graduates had been leaders in the national development of science; education; engineering; exploration; public works; business; manufacturing; communications; and transportation. Thanks in considerable part to West Point, when World War I ended, the United States was no longer a developing nation but an established world power.

West Point Cadet Douglas MacArthur and his mother, Mary Pinkney Hardy MacArthur. His father, Maj. Gen. Arthur MacArthur, soon to become the army's highest-ranking officer, remained in the Philippines when his son entered West Point in 1899. His mother, however, took up a four-year residence in West Point's Thayer Hotel.

DOUGLAS MacARTHUR

1880–1964   Class of 1903

An outstanding cadet, MacArthur left the Academy for a variety of engineering and staff positions. In 1917, he sailed to France as chief of staff of the 42nd Division. Later its commander, he was twice wounded and much decorated.

Appointed superintendent of West Point after the war, he instituted reforms in curriculum, teaching methods, and standards of performance that began to restore West Point to an academic respectability badly eroded by wartime policies.

After various command assignments and a five-year tour as army chief of staff, MacArthur returned to the Philippines in 1935 to organize and train the Filipino army. Recalled to active duty in World War II, he led American and allied forces in the Pacific to victory over Japan. He remained as military governor of the country and ended his career as commander of United Nations forces in the Korean War (1950–1953).

> **"***A general is just as good or as bad as the troops under his command make him.***"**

DOUGLAS MacARTHUR TO CONGRESS, 20 AUGUST 1962

THE CLASS THE STARS FELL ON

THE West Point graduating class of 1915 numbered 164. More than a third of that extraordinary class won stars, 59 in all—twenty-four brigadier generals (one star), twenty-four major generals (two stars), seven lieutenant generals (three stars), two generals (four stars), and two generals of the armies (five stars).

The two who attained the army's highest possible rank, general of the armies, were Dwight David Eisenhower and Omar Nelson Bradley. They joined a very select group. Before World War II only four men had held that rank: Ulysses S. Grant (Class of 1843); William T. Sherman (Class of 1840); Philip H. Sheridan (Class of 1853); and John J. Pershing (Class of 1886).

Three others attained the rank during World War II. One, George C. Marshall, was not a West Pointer—he graduated from the Virginia Military Institute—but the other two were: Douglas MacArthur (Class of 1903) and Henry H. Arnold (Class of 1907). There have been no others since.

J.J. Pershing's four-star epaulette. Pershing refused the fifth star to which he was entitled.

OMAR NELSON BRADLEY

1893–1981   Class of 1915

Until 1943, when Bradley took command of II Corps in North Africa, he had never seen combat. Most of his army life had been spent learning or teaching about war. But given the chance, Bradley showed himself to be one of those indispensable right hands, like Jackson or Sherman, who make the grand strategy of a Lee, a Grant, or an Eisenhower work.

With Eisenhower as supreme commander, Bradley advanced from corps commander in North Africa and Sicily to command the First Army in the Normandy invasion, then the 12th Army Group in the victory over Germany. No other general in American history commanded so many troops in the field —1.3 million—as Bradley did in 1945.

After the war, Bradley headed the Veterans Administration, then succeeded Eisenhower as army chief of staff. He later became the first chairman of the new joint chiefs of staff.

> **❝** *... [T]he wrong war, at the wrong place, at the wrong time, and with the wrong enemy.* **❞**
>
> OMAR N. BRADLEY, TESTIMONY TO CONGRESS ON THE KOREAN WAR, 15 MAY 1951

Bradley lettered in baseball three times at West Point. He appears second from left in this photo of the 1914 team. Every member of the team who remained in the army became a general.

Dwight D. Eisenhower
(Class of 1915) lettered
in football at West Point.

MAKING THE MODERN ACADEMY

WEST Point's near collapse in World War I was not repeated in World War II, but the Academy faced serious postwar challenges. Its persistent dilemma was balancing a four-year undergraduate education with the training of professional military officers. The problem became acute after World War II as officers' roles expanded into many nonmilitary areas at the same time that technical demands multiplied.

Maxwell D. Taylor (Class of 1922) became superintendent in late 1945. He updated and expanded the curriculum, adding courses in the humanities and social studies, and brought in outside speakers. But it was the 1956 arrival of Garrison Davidson (Class of 1927) as superintendent that began a definitive new reform era. Davidson's proposals and the ferment he initiated produced the greatest transformation of the West Point curriculum since Sylvanus Thayer in the early 19th century.

Portrait of Maxwell Taylor by Bjorn Peter Egeli, oil on canvas (detail)

GARRISON HOLT DAVIDSON

1904–1992   Class of 1927

When Major General Davidson returned to West Point in 1956 as superintendent, his reputation as the Academy's successful prewar football coach and an outstanding soldier in both World War II and the Korean War preceded him. Having just spent two years leading the army's Command and General Staff College, he firmly believed that a changing world demanded major changes at West Point. Politically astute and well informed, he became the Academy's most successful reformer since Thayer.

Davidson's foremost achievement was introducing electives to the curriculum. No longer would all cadets follow exactly the same program. He also revitalized the honor code, de-emphasizing football and promoting athletic participation by all cadets. His four-year term was not enough to accomplish all he wished. His offer to forgo a third star and stay for another term to finish what he had begun was not accepted, but others carried on West Point's continuing transformation.

CREIGHTON WILLIAMS ABRAMS, JR.

1914–1974 ★ Class of 1936

Commissioned in the cavalry after graduation, Abrams switched to armor in 1940. In 1943 he assumed command of the 37th Tank Battalion of the 4th Armored Division, which landed in Normandy a month after D-Day. His battalion spearheaded General Patton's Third Army across Europe. Abrams emerged from World War II a much-decorated colonel, regarded as one of the army's best tank commanders.

Largely unknown outside the army, Abrams rose through increasingly responsible positions to four-star rank. His greatest challenge came when he took command of American forces in Vietnam in 1968. For four years he oversaw Vietnamization, a policy of arming, training, and strengthening the South Vietnamese army to assume full responsibility for national defense as U.S. forces gradually withdrew. The process was incomplete when Abrams left in 1972 to become the army's chief of staff. The army Abrams (M1) battle tank is named for him.

66 *I'm supposed to be the best tank commander in the army, but I have one peer—Abe Abrams.* **99**

GEN. GEORGE S. PATTON, JR., JULY 1944

Gen. Abrams (right), commanding U.S. forces in Vietnam, confers with Gen. George I. Forsythe, commander of the 1st Cavalry Division, in Phuoc Vinh, 1968.

BENJAMIN OLIVER DAVIS Jr.

1912–2002 · Class of 1936

Davis was West Point's fourth African American graduate and the first in the 20th century. Like the others, he endured four years of racial prejudice. In the Cadet Chapel two weeks after graduation he married Agatha Scott, his much-needed support in the coming years of struggle against racial discrimination within and beyond the military community.

Ordered to Tuskegee Institute, Alabama, for segregated flight training in World War II, Davis completed the course and took command of the all-black 99th Pursuit Squadron, the famous Tuskegee Airmen. He emerged from the war a much decorated colonel. Military segregation ended by presidential order in 1949.

In 1954 Davis became the air force's first black general, just as his father earlier had been the army's first. He retired in 1970 as lieutenant general. In a 1998 ceremony at the White House, President Clinton awarded the 86-year-old Davis his fourth star.

Benjamin Davis (far left) with Tuskegee Airmen

❝*I do not find it complimentary to me or to the nation to be called 'the first black West Point graduate in this century.'*❞

BENJAMIN O. DAVIS, JR., *BENJAMIN O. DAVIS, JR., AMERICAN: AN AUTOBIOGRAPHY*, 1991

THE CLASS OF 1980

FOLLOWING congressional passage of the Equal Rights Amendment in 1972, West Point began preparing contingency plans for admitting women. The end of the draft and shift to a volunteer army underscored the need for change. In 1975 Congress enacted, and President Ford signed into law, a measure requiring the service academies to admit women in 1976. Perceived and argued as an issue of simple fairness, the change had wide public support.

West Point committed itself to making integration a success. Recognizing the importance of beginning with a substantial number of women, West Point immediately began active recruiting. Of 148 women offered admission, 119 became members of the class of 1980.

At first, groups of eight to ten women were assigned to twelve (of thirty-six) cadet companies. By late the following year, all cadet companies included women. Doubts about their ability to meet West Point's rigorous standards, and even some hostility from male cadets, soon subsided. Within little more than a decade, women had occupied every leadership role in the Corps of Cadets from squad leader to cadet first captain.

Female cadets

The class of 1980 was the first West Point graduating class
to include female cadets.

INDEX

PICTURE CREDITS